Baptist Questions, Baptist Answers

Exploring Christian Faith

Bill J. Leonard

WESTMINSTER
JOHN KNOX PRESS
LOUISVILLE · KENTUCKY

© 2009 Bill J. Leonard

Book design by Sharon Adams
Cover design by Night & Day Design

First edition
Published by Westminster John Knox Press
Louisville, Kentucky

This book is printed on acid-free paper that meets the American National Standards Institute Z39.48 standard. ∞

PRINTED IN THE UNITED STATES OF AMERICA

Library of Congress Cataloging-in-Publication Data

Leonard, Bill (Bill J.)
    Baptist questions, Baptist answers : exploring Christian faith / Bill J. Leonard. — 1st ed.
        p. cm.
    Includes bibliographical references and index.
    ISBN 978-0-664-23289-4 (alk. paper)
    1. Baptists—Doctrines I. Title.
BX6331.3.L46 2009
286—dc221

                                                          2008034407

To the members of First Baptist Church, Highland Avenue,
Winston-Salem, North Carolina,
and the members of Myers Park Baptist Church,
Charlotte, North Carolina,

who continually welcome me to worship and a celebration of grace
and, in very diverse and wonderful ways,
keep me Baptist.

Contents

14 Polity   111

For Further Reading   121

Welcome to the Book

Asking Questions

"Are we there yet?" children often ask their parents fifteen minutes after the three-hour car trip has begun. The question is both logistical and lively, a sign of impatience and curiosity all at once. We all want to know when we will arrive, what the end of things might be, and how we are going to get there. So it is with faith. We ask questions of God, Bible, church, and culture in order to understand the nature of faith, the reasons for believing, the content of belief itself, and the relevance of faith for life and death. Our inquiries are sometimes naïve, sometimes ironic, sometimes immediate, sometimes enduring, and sometimes panicked. And the answers—where do they come from, who is qualified to offer them, and what do we do when they are not sufficient? But before we get to the answers, perhaps we need to ask, Who makes up the questions?

This book on Baptist questions and answers begins with two small but significant disclaimers. First, Baptists are such a diverse group, with such a historic tradition for dissent, that no one Baptist should presume to speak for any other, let alone all, Baptists. Indeed, many of the "answers" offered in any text on Baptists may prove insufficient for some readers from specific segments of the Baptist family. The tired old saw that "where there are four Baptists, there will be at least five opinions" still holds considerable weight in the Baptist world. One seemingly universal trait of Baptist history and practice can all too readily be contradicted by a specific Baptist individual or community. Even those questions thought to be essential may have varying degrees of nuance for certain Baptist believers and denominational subgroups. We must proceed with caution in raising the questions, let alone in providing the "answers."

Likewise, Baptists are so divided over issues of theology, polity, and ministry that there are no doubt some readers who will object to my being chosen to address these questions/answers, preferring a more "orthodox" representative from across the theological spectrum. I enter this endeavor with caution and an aim at objectivity where possible, amid my own commitments to a Baptist "conscience." In a time of permanent transition in American, indeed global, religious life, I remain irrepressibly a Baptist, bound to a tradition that is questionable and exemplary all at once. I have learned much from my Baptist forbears and am grateful for most of the lessons.

Second, any effort to articulate Baptist responses to important questions of identity, belief, and practice must begin by acknowledging that historically Baptist tradition essentially begins at both ends of the classic Protestant theological spectrum. That is, by the 1630s there were two distinct groups of Baptists, one Arminian and the other Calvinist in perspective, each reflecting differing if not contradictory approaches to the essentials of the faith. Later Baptists, like many other groups, divided in multiple ways over fundamentalist, conservative, moderate, and liberal interpretations of these basic Christian doctrines and actions. In the United States, the Baptist tradition includes large numbers of Caucasian and African American Baptists whose communities both agree and differ significantly over the nature of the church and its mission in the world. Given that diversity of theology and praxis, questions and answers related to "Baptistness" inevitably require serious qualification.

This Book

This book offers a snapshot of what seems to me to be certain essential questions for understanding the life and teaching of the people called Baptists. Much of the format and many of the questions raised here parallel those in two earlier similar volumes: *Presbyterian Questions, Presbyterian Answers* by Donald McKim, and *United Methodist Questions, United Methodist Answers* by F. Belton Joyner Jr. I am grateful to both of them for the insights offered in their books.

The specific questions offered here represent my attempt to summarize essential elements of Baptist belief and practice, and to provide "answers" that reflect the commonality and diversity of Baptist ideas on specific topics. I draw on historic statements, common commitments, and subgroup distinctions in my attempt to generalize about shared beliefs and to qualify differences where necessary. Thus, I rely extensively on Baptist confessions of faith, those basic statements of doctrine of varying lengths, many written in the seventeenth century. Nonetheless, these documents in themselves reflect theological diversity, indeed contradiction, among Baptists that was present from the beginning. Because Baptists are so diverse, it may be helpful to use their historic confessional documents, particularly those written in the seventeenth century, to get at the rudimentary elements of Baptist belief and identity. I rely on the confessions because they represent a small consensus of the earliest Baptist communities, though I know full well that many Baptists are hesitant to use any "man-made" document as indicative of what they have or should have believed. The confessions used here illustrate classic Baptist diversity amid a commonality of belief and practice that characterizes a genuinely distinct movement. If I had departed from these historic documents to describe Baptist beliefs, there would have been no end to this book.

I also know that some potential readers of this text will insist that one who departs from their particular theological or ecclesiological perspective on the nature of Baptist identity cannot be considered Baptist at all. This surely includes varying views on the inspiration of Holy Scripture, the atonement and/or second coming of Jesus Christ, the social gospel, the nature of baptism, the priesthood of all believers, the role of women in ministry, and the separation of church and state. At the same time, I am well aware that many Baptist congregations, old and new, conservative and liberal, are at this moment minimizing the Baptist name and its accompanying ethos. For some postmoderns, Baptist questions and Baptist answers are just not that important.

For my part, as both a Baptist preacher and a historian of the Baptists, such questions continue to be significant and are especially relevant to an era when a worrisome form of generic Christianity threatens to undermine serious conversation about the hard questions of the nature and future of the church. Whether churches continue to claim the name Baptist, they will have to deal with these questions sooner or later if they want to pass on identity to a new generation of "baptized believers" who find their way into Baptist congregations.

One final word. I commend Westminster John Knox Press for publishing a book such as this at this point in time. By my calculations (and of course not all Baptist historians agree about this), 2009 represents the 400th anniversary of the Baptist entry into the world. The little band of English Separatist Puritans who gathered in the "bake-house" in Amsterdam and received believers' baptism did so sometime in 1609 (so some of us calculate). I am honored to celebrate their heritage in print and to acknowledge the debt I bear to their courage, their insight, their faith in God, and their opposition to religious establishments. Many of that group died in prison or in exile as a result of their courage and convictions regarding religious liberty and freedom of conscience. I hope to have such courage when the time comes.

Sources

Sources for this brief volume include a number of primary and secondary sources relative to Baptist ideas and ideals. Confessions of faith are found in William L. Lumpkin's invaluable study *Baptist Confessions of Faith* (Valley Forge, PA: Judson Press, 1974). Other primary source documents are found in H. Leon McBeth, *A Sourcebook for Baptist Heritage* (Nashville: Broadman Press, 1987; William Brackney, ed., *Baptist Life and Thought* (Valley

Forge, PA: Judson Press, 1983; and Curtis Freeman, et al., *Baptist Roots* (Valley Forge, PA: Judson Press, 1999). Secondary sources include H. Leon McBeth, *The Baptist Heritage* (Nashville: Broadman Press, 1987); William Brackney, *The Baptists* (New York: Greenwood Press, 1988); and W. Glenn Jonas, *The Baptist River* (Macon, GA: Mercer University Press, 2006). I also continue to use the sources in that classic work *American Christianity: An Historical Interpretation with Representative Documents,* edited by H. Shelton Smith, Robert T. Handy, and Lefferts A. Loetscher, 2 volumes (New York: Charles Scribner's Sons, 1963), and another classic source collection edited by Henry Bettenson, *Documents of the Christian Church* (London: Oxford University Press, 1963).

Some may find my own books—*Baptist Ways: A History* (Valley Forge, PA: Judson Press, 2003), *Baptists in America* (New York: Columbia University Press, 2005), and *A Dictionary of Baptists in America* (Downers Grove, IL: InterVarsity Press, 1994)—helpful for further studies.

How to Use this Book

I hope that congregations and individuals will find this a good resource for basic information about the Baptists. It could be of value for specific classes, especially for new members or for those approaching baptism in Baptist churches. It might be used on retreats in a concentrated study of Baptist belief and practice. The text could also offer a brief survey of Baptist identity for those who simply want to answer the question "Why are we Baptists?" and might be beneficial for recommendation to laity who want a brief overview of basic Baptist beliefs. I hope that students of the Baptist experience will find this book a valuable place to begin or continue their studies.

1

Baptist History and Heritage

1. Who are the Baptists?

Theories of Baptist origins abound. Some believe that Baptists can be traced all the way back to Jesus' baptism in River Jordan by John the Baptizer, a direct lineage of true New Testament churches. Others suggest a "kinship" with the Radical Reformation Anabaptists who promoted believers' baptism and a free church tradition in the early days of the Protestant Reformation. Still others, I am among them, trace the origins to the seventeenth-century Puritans and their efforts to recover New Testament Christianity beyond the state churches and sectarian clamor of post-Reformation Europe.

So let us suggest that Baptists are a second-generation Protestant communion that began around 1609 with a group of English Separatist Puritans exiled in Amsterdam. This group determined that the church should be composed of believers only and that baptism should be given only after persons profess faith in Christ. The earliest Baptists were Arminian in their theology, appropriating the theology of the Dutch theologian Jacob Arminius (1560–1609). Their belief that Christ's death on the cross was for the sins of the entire world and that all persons were potentially elected to salvation led to their designation as General Baptists. By the 1630s a second group of Baptists had developed in England. Known as Particular Baptists because of their Calvinist theology, they believed that Christ's death was applicable only to the elect, whom God had chosen for salvation before the foundation of the world.

God's irresistible grace would draw the elect to salvation, overcoming their total depravity and keeping them until the end. Thus, from a historical perspective, Baptists begin at both ends of the theological spectrum with Arminian and Calvinist groups that inform much Baptist life and thought to this day.

In the twenty-first century Baptists claim a worldwide constituency of over forty million persons, with approximately thirty million living in North America. In the United States there are more than sixty different groups that claim the name Baptist in some form or another.

2. What beliefs and practices are basic to all Baptists?

Baptists share many beliefs, even when they define those common doctrines a bit differently. These classic "Baptist distinctives" include the following:

1. Biblical authority is normative for faith and practice.
2. The church is a community of believers who can testify to an experience of grace through faith in Christ.
3. Baptism is administered to those who testify to faith and is by immersion.
4. Baptism and the Lord's Supper are the two "ordinances" (some early Baptists said "sacraments") of the church. (Some Baptists add footwashing to that list.)
5. The authority of Christ is mediated through the congregation of believers. Each congregation has the autonomy to determine its ministry and method.
6. Congregations may join together in "associations" of churches for mutual ministry and fellowship.
7. The priesthood of all believers means that all baptized believers are "called" to minister to others in the world. Both laity and clergy are called to minister in the church and the world.
8. Certain persons are "set aside" for the ministry of the Word and pastoral service in the church.
9. Religious liberty should be normative in the state.
10. Liberty of conscience means that believers can be trusted to

interpret Scripture aright in the context of community under the guidance of the Holy Spirit.

This is not to suggest that all Baptists agree on what these ideas mean biblically and theologically. Rather, they represent certain distinguishing marks of identity that are applied variously by Baptist groups and individuals.

 ### 3. What are some of the Baptist groups in the United States?

The Baptist family in the United States is vast and diverse. The following are but a few of the groups that claim the Baptist name in some form or another. They occupy various theological and historical positions and are located in various regions and cultures across the country.

1. *American Baptist Churches in the U.S.A.* (ABC USA): Numbering about one million members this group dates its beginnings with the founding of the General Convention of the Baptist Denomination for Foreign Missions in 1814. Spread throughout the United States, with particular strength in the Midwest and West, the ABC was earlier known as the Northern Baptist Convention and the American Baptist Convention.

2. *Southern Baptist Convention* (SBC): Founded in 1845 in a dispute over slavery between Baptists in the North and South, the SBC is the largest Baptist (and Protestant) denomination in the United States with some sixteen million members. Conservative in theology, its primary strength remains in the South and Southwest.

3. *African American Baptists:* Major African American Baptist denominations include the National Baptist Convention of the U.S.A., Inc.; the National Baptist Convention of America, Unincorporated; the Progressive National Baptist Convention; and the National Missionary Baptist Convention. African Americans came into the Baptist tradition during slavery under the influence of revivals and camp meetings in the South and Southwest. Debates over such things as denominational ownership of property,

improvement of working conditions, and the authority of denominational leaders led to various divisions among black Baptist groups in the United States.

4. *Appalachian Baptists:* These include several Baptist groups, most of which are Calvinist in one form or another. They are identified with names such as the Primitive, Old Regular, United, and Union Baptists. One small but fascinating faith community is known as the Primitive Baptist Universalists, popularly but mistakenly called the "No Hellers" because they believe that ultimately all persons will be saved. Appalachian Baptists came into the mountains during the eighteenth and ninteenth centuries, tend toward various types of Calvinism, and give little or no attention to direct missionary efforts, Sunday schools, or a paid ministry. Their numbers are generally in decline, but their sense of witness to New Testament orthodoxy is as strong as ever.

5. *Landmark Baptists:* "Old Landmarkists" insist that Baptists began with Jesus' baptism by John the Baptist and can trace their lineage through multiple Baptist groups in church history. These dissenting communions—Montanists, Donatists, Cathari, Waldensians, Anabaptists, and Baptists—were "Baptist in everything but name," offering a succession of Baptist churches all the way from the New Testament to the present. Landmark groups include the Baptist Missionary Association, the American Baptist Association, and various fundamentalist-related Baptist groups. Generally fundamentalist in their theology, Landmark Baptists are strong in the South and Southwest, especially in Oklahoma, Arkansas, and Texas.

6. *Fundamentalist Baptists:* Many Baptists hold fundamentalist beliefs regarding biblical inerrancy, Christ's virgin birth, as well as his bodily resurrection and second coming. Most of these groups are suspicious of denominational alignments and prefer to associate in "fellowships" of pastors. Adherents to these Baptist communions number several million, and several ministerial "fellowships" include the Southwide Baptist Fellowship, the World Fundamentalist Association, and the Bible Baptist Fellowship.

7. *Conservative Baptist Association of America:* This group broke away from the American Baptist Convention in the 1940s

over issues related to fundamentalism and liberalism. The denomination maintains various collective ministries, including certain missionary-sending organizations, and two theological seminaries.

8. *Ethnic Baptists:* Immigrant Baptist groups formed early in America. These include the Baptist General Conference formed in 1852 by Swedish immigrants, the North American Baptist Conference formed by German Baptists in 1843, and the Norwegian Baptist Conference founded in 1910 (and disbanded in 1954).

9. *Recent Baptist Groups:* The Alliance of Baptists, founded in 1986, and the Cooperative Baptist Fellowship, formed in 1991, are two Baptist groups formed by churches and individuals who left the Southern Baptist Convention as a result of disputes over biblical inerrancy and denominational control. They represent a more "moderate" coalitions of Baptists who moved away from the increasing fundamentalist orientation of the Southern Baptist Convention.

10. *Reformed Baptists:* Represented in various subgroups, Reformed Baptists have developed renewed energy in many churches through a resurgence of classic Calvinism. They represent an effort to reassert Calvinist doctrine and practice in Baptist churches new and old.

4. Why are there so many Baptist groups?

"Baptists multiply by dividing," the old saying goes. Truth is, Baptist polity combines with theological diversity to create the possibility, if not the probability, for carrying out the gospel in a variety of Baptist-related ways. Baptist groups were formed as a result of historic causes (missions or antimissions), schism over doctrinal and social issues (slavery or fundamentalism/liberalism), ethnic and regional identity (German, Norwegian, African American, Hispanic, or Landmark), and internal disputes (denominational control, ministerial authority, congregational autonomy). Baptist differences over Calvinism and Arminianism mean that there are multiple approaches to understanding the nature of faith and salvation. Congregational church government means that Baptist churches may be started by a local group of believers without asking permission from any other governing body, whether bishops, presbyteries, synods, or conferences. Churches can be connected to larger Baptist denominations or associations or stand alone.

5. What individuals shaped the Baptist movement?

Baptists have no single, prominent historical founders such as Martin Luther, John Calvin, or John Wesley. Some of their early leaders died in prison or in exile while others only remained Baptists for a short period of time. Such was the case with *John Smyth* and *Thomas Helwys,* the two prominent founders of the first Baptist church in Amsterdam in 1609. Smyth (d. 1612) was educated at Cambridge and ordained an Anglican priest. Moving through Puritan Separatism he claimed Baptist views on the nature of a believers' church and baptized the first group of Baptists. Shortly thereafter he left the Baptists for the Mennonites. Thomas Helwys (c. 1550–c. 1615) was trained in the law, helped underwrite the English exiles in Amsterdam, and brought them back to England. His work A Short Declaration of *the Mystery of Iniquity* (1612) was one of the first calls for complete religious liberty written in English. He died in prison.

Puritan preacher/theologian *Roger Williams* (1603–1683) and physician *Dr. John Clarke* (1609–1676) were instrumental in founding the first Baptist churches in America, one at Providence and the other at Newport, Rhode Island. Williams, the quintessential dissenter, introduced significant issues of religious liberty into Baptist life but only remained a Baptist for a short time. Clarke spent much of his life working to secure the charter for the Rhode Island colony with freedom of religion as its centerpiece. *Isaac Backus* (1724–1806) was a New England Baptist pastor who lobbied for religious liberty at the first Continental Congress.

William Carey (1761–1834) was one of the leaders in the modern global mission movement. Carey insisted that it was the "duty" of Baptists to take the gospel to the "heathen"; he set out for India in 1793 and spent his life teaching, preaching, and translating the Scripture into indigenous Indian languages. *Adoniram Judson* (1788–1850) and his spouse, *Ann Hasseltine Judson* (1789–1826), were the first American Baptist missionaries. Sent out as the Congregational missionaries to India, they accepted Baptist views on shipboard and requested funding for a new Baptist endeavor in Burma. Their request led to the founding of the General Missionary Convention of the Baptist Denomination in the United States in 1814, the first national mission society founded by U.S. Baptists. Both Judsons became models for missionary service among Protestants in general and Baptists in particular.

George Leile (c. 1750–1800) was another former slave who helped to found the Silver Bluff Baptist Church, probably the first African American Baptist Church in North America, sometime in the 1770s. He became the first Baptist missionary to Jamaica. *Lott Carey* (1780–1829) was a former slave who was the first African American Baptist sent as a missionary to West Africa. He organized churches and was even named interim governor of Liberia.

Henrietta Hall Shuck (1817–1844) joined her husband, *J. Lewis Shuck* (1814–1863), in traveling to China in 1834 as missionaries sent by the American Baptist Foreign Mission Society. She founded a girls' school and wrote extensively about missionary work in China. *Mary Webb* (1779–1861) was born in Boston, where she experienced a childhood illness that left her with severe physical disabilities. A member of Second Baptist Church, she led in founding the Boston Female Society for Missionary Purposes, the first women's mission organization in the United States. It united Baptist and Congregationalist women in raising funds for mission activities at home and abroad. *Charlotte (Lottie) Moon* (1840–1912) was one of the first single women sent to China by the Foreign Mission Board of the Southern Baptist Convention. She taught extensively in remote areas of China, insisting that women should be given more freedom to evangelize and have greater authority to do their own work.

In the twentieth and twenty-first centuries, the diversity of the

Baptists is no more clearly illustrated than in the political and religious leaders who identified themselves as Baptists. These include civil rights leaders such as Reverends *Martin Luther King Jr.*, *Fred Shuttlesworth* (Birmingham, Alabama), *Gardner Taylor* (Concord Baptist Church, New York), and *Jesse Jackson*. Megachurch Baptists include *Rick Warren, Bishop Eddie Long, Charles Stanley, Ed Young Sr., and Ed Young Jr.*, among others. Democrats include former presidents *Jimmy Carter* and *Bill Clinton*, as well as former vice president and Nobel laureate *Al Gore*. Republicans include former senators *Strom Thurman* and *Jesse Helms* as well as presidential candidate *Mike Huckabee*. Baptist women in the public square include the late congresswoman *Barbara Jordan*, poet *Maya Angelou*, and the children's advocate *Marian Wright Edelman*.

 6. How do Baptists get along with others?

Throughout much of their history, many Baptists have resisted cooperation with other non-Baptist groups. Some of this was the result of the Landmark belief that Baptists alone were the "one true church" on earth and that autonomous Baptist churches should not engage with denominational "hierarchies." Many frontier Baptists worked with other Protestants in the camp meetings and revivals on the frontier, but as denominations took shape, they turned to greater competition. Certain fundamentalist Baptist groups are hesitant to cooperate with other Baptist and non-Baptist communions that seem less strenuous on orthodox dogmas ("To know a liberal is to be a liberal"). Although the American Baptist Churches, U.S.A., the Seventh Day Baptists, and some of the National Baptist bodies are members of the World and National Councils of Churches, many other Baptist groups have rejected membership lest local autonomy of individual churches be compromised. Many Baptist groups maintain membership in the Baptist World Alliance (BWA), a fellowship of Baptist bodies and individuals worldwide.

Many liberal and conservative Baptists have forged alliances with non-Baptist individuals and churches in a variety of denominational and nondenominational congregations, linked together by common belief in or concern over biblical interpretation, theological uniformity, mission endeavors, and varying ways of understanding the nature of religious freedom.

2

God

7. How do we know God?

"In the beginning God . . ."—so Gen. 1:1 introduces the Hebrew Scriptures, and the Christian texts echo that affirmation with the writer of Hebrews' words that we believe God "is and . . . is a rewarder of them that diligently seek him" (Heb. 11:6 KJV). God is present in creation and draws near to those who are thus created. Like their Catholic and Protestant counterparts, Baptists start with the assertion that God exists and is the author of both creation and salvation. The First London Confession of Faith, written by Particular Baptists in 1644, begins with a statement on the nature of God:

> That God as he is in himself, cannot be comprehended of any but himself, dwelling in that inaccessible light, that no eye can attain unto, whom never man saw, nor can see; that there is but one God, one Christ, one Spirit, one Faith, one Baptism; one Rule of holiness and obedience for all Saints, at all times, in all places to be observed. (Lumpkin, 156)

Baptists thus insist that God is not only "knowable" but that God seeks us out and is ready for fellowship whenever it is offered by the faithful. Perhaps it is less a question of our knowing God than it is an abiding assertion that "God knows us."

Faith in God begins with mystery and transcendence. As the hymn declares,

> Immortal, invisible, God only wise;
> In light inaccessible, hid from our eyes

God is separate from us, above us, beyond us, outside us. Yet for reasons we cannot fully comprehend, God has chosen to come to us, most clearly in Jesus Christ, God's "only begotten Son." In Christ, the Unknowable One has become known. Thus, if Baptists begin with God, they continue with God's revelation in Jesus Christ. In the mystery of God's existence, Baptists sing the rest of the hymn:

> Most blessed, most glorious, the Ancient of Days
> Almighty, victorious, Thy great name we praise!

8. What does it mean to speak of God as "the Trinity"?

One of the great and mystifying truths of Christian faith is the idea of the Trinity as a way of describing the nature of God and establishing a means of talking about God's self-revelation. In an early Declaration of Faith written from Amsterdam in 1611, the founders of the Baptist movement asserted, "There are THREE which bear record in heaven, the FATHER, the WORD [Jesus Christ], and the SPIRIT; and these THREE are one GOD, in all equality, I John 5:7; Philippians 2:5–6. By whom all things are created and preserved, in Heaven and in Earth. Genesis I chapter" (Lumpkin, 117).

With a few notable exceptions (some eighteenth-century Baptists held Unitarian views), Baptists are unashamed Trinitarians, insisting that God is revealed as Father, Son, and Holy Spirit, expressed to the church as Creator, Redeemer, and Sustainer. They readily sing the words of Nicene orthodoxy in the popular hymn "Holy, Holy, Holy, Merciful and Mighty; God in three persons, blessed Trinity." Although most do not use the Nicene Creed, they would nonetheless acquiesce to its orthodoxy as evident in the words of the First London Confession:

In this God-head, there is the Father, the Son, and the Spirit;
being every one of them one and the same God; and therefore
not divided, but distinguished one from another by their several
properties; the Father being from himself, the Son of the Father
from everlasting, the Holy spirit proceeding from the Father and
the Son. (Lumpkin, 156–57)

These formal statements illustrate the technical, doctrinal
approach to Trinitarian theology that is characteristic of Baptist
thought, as well as that of other Christians. The Trinity is thus an
essential way of understanding the way the transcendent God is made
known in creation, salvation, and continuing presence in the church
and in the world. The "division" facilitates the unity, and the unity is
not shattered by the distinctive nature of God's self-revelation.

But theological categories are not the only way Baptists think
and act on Trinitarian concepts. Popular piety and practice lead
many Baptists to interpret the nature of the Trinity primarily in
terms of the centrality of Jesus Christ, the agent of conversion and
new life. In other words, many Baptists would simply say that "in
order to know what God is like, we look at Jesus." Theologically,
therefore, God's essential benevolence, desire to save, and continuing activity in the world is revealed in Jesus, the fullest revelation
of the nature of God. While Baptists do indeed sing, "God, our
Father, we adore thee; we, Thy children, bless Thy name," they
may also (and more often) sing, "Jesus is the sweetest name I
know; and He's just the same, as his lovely name; and that's the
reason why I love him so. Oh, Jesus is the sweetest name I know."

9. What is God's relationship with humanity?

In their understanding of God's relationship with humanity,
Baptists generally follow various forms of a theology of "the fall"
as set forth by the fourth-century theologian Augustine and echoed
later in distinctive ways by Reformers such as John Calvin and
Jacob Arminius. In essence this means that God created human
beings for fellowship and freedom but that they chose to break the

rules, and their sinful natures—passed on variously to each generation—continue to bring separation. In an effort to restore the relationship with fallen humanity, God ultimately sent his "only
begotten Son" to save the world. The Declaration of Faith of English People (1611) sums it up this way:

> Men are by nature the Children of wrath, Ephesians 2:3, born in
> iniquity and in sin conceived, Psalm 51:5. Wise to all evil, but
> to good they have no knowledge, Jeremiah 4:22. *The natural
> man perceiveth not the things of the Spirit of God,* I Corinthians
> 2:14. [In spite of having] "no disposition or will unto any good,"
> [through Christ humans] "may receive grace, or may reject
> grace, according to that saying; Deut. 30:19. *I call Heaven and
> earth to record. This day against you, that I have set before you
> life and death, blessing and cursing: Therefore choose life, that
> both thou and thy seed may live"* (Lumpkin, 117–18).

Baptists thus agree that human beings need saving in order to
be restored to a relationship with God. Their disagreement
involves the nature of individual eligibility for such saving grace.
Calvinist Baptists believe that only the elect, chosen before the
world's foundation, will ultimately receive the grace of restoration
and reconciliation with God. More Arminian-leaning Baptists suggest that all persons are potentially "elected" to salvation but only
those who come on the terms of election—repentance and faith—
will actually secure the restored relationship with God through
Christ. Sooner or later, those who have cast themselves on Christ
for salvation must face the reality that some are not chosen and
struggle with the possibility that it might have been one of them.
Casting ourselves on Christ and receiving salvation or damnation
from him is the basic question confronting at least some church
members today.

 **10. If God is "in control" of the world, why is there so
much suffering?**

This question opens the door to the issue of "theodicy," that
ancient quest for why suffering exists in a world created and

guided by a benevolent God. It is asked in ways such as "Why do the innocent suffer?" or, most basically, "Why do bad things happen to good people?" Is all suffering and catastrophe somehow "God's will"? Does God "permit" everything that happens in the world? Responses to these questions may include issues surrounding the "providence" of God, which means the way God works or does not work in the world.

The Second London Confession of Faith, published by Particular Baptists in 1688, follows the strong Calvinist orientation of the more-Presbyterian Westminster Confession of the 1640s. The Second London Confession is clear about God's providential control, noting that

> God, the good *Creator* of all things, in his infinite power, and wisdom, doth uphold, direct, dispose, and govern all Creatures, and things, from the greatest even to the least, by *his* most wise and holy providence, to the end for that which they were *created;* according unto his infallible foreknowledge, and the free and immutable Counsel of his own will. (Lumpkin, 256)

Given the belief in God's overarching providence in all things, the confession concludes that "whatsoever befalls any of [God's] elect is by his appointment, for his glory, and their good" (Lumpkin, 251).

The Orthodox Creed written by General Baptists in 1679 is much more concise than Second London, simply stating,

> The Almighty God, that created all things, and gave them their being, by his infinite power and wisdom, doth sustain and uphold, and move, direct, dispose, and govern all creatures and things, from the greatest to the least, according to the counsel of his own good will and pleasure, for his own glory, and his creatures' good. (Lumpkin, 305)

When it comes to God's providential care, Baptists have varying views. While most would agree that it is God's world and not a sparrow falls without God's knowledge, they do not always agree on God's direct activity, often distinguishing between God's "intentional" will and God's "permissive" will. In other words, God intends certain things, such as redemption, and God permits other things related to world events, natural disasters, and human circumstances. Still other Baptists would suggest that God sends rain to "the just and the unjust" (Matt. 5:45), and the gift of God is the strength of the Spirit's presence in times of difficulty as well as celebration. God shares in our suffering and struggle. The incarnation is evidence that "nobody knows the trouble I've seen; nobody knows but Jesus."

 11. What is the role of God in the creation of the world?

$\mathbf{S}$ince the publication of Charles Darwin's *Origin of Species* (1859) Baptists, like other Protestants, have divided over the relationship between "science and the Bible," or "evolution and creationism," or, more recently, "evolution and creation science." A significant number of Baptists support the Genesis account of creation as the foundation of God's activity in the world, forming it *fiat* (from nothing), speaking light, land, and living beings into existence quite literally, although often differing as to the interpretation of a "day" in the creation stories. Others remain committed to the biblical account but link it with "creationist" or "creation science" interpretations, insisting that the theory of evolution is simply that, a theory that should be included along with other explanations of the nature of beginnings. Still other Baptists would identify themselves with "theistic evolution," attributing the creative impetus to the Divine while affirming that Darwinian evolutionary synthesis or something like it appears to be the method God chose to accomplish creative intentions. Others, perhaps a smaller number, assert that belief in God and scientific views of evolution are distinct issues that may be maintained but need not be forced into collaboration. These debates show no signs of ending. Indeed, they have become so intense that many younger Baptists (certainly not all) are beginning to look to other issues for how Christians might work together, even as they disagree on these basic ideas of creation.

Faith and science, reason and revelation collide with considerable impact among Baptist congregations and individuals today, often about the very nature of God. Amid these divisions, perhaps we can still sing together, "This is my Father's world, and to my listening ears, all nature sings and round me rings, the music of the spheres."

3

Jesus Christ

12. Who is Jesus Christ?

Baptists are profoundly Christocentric (Christ-centered) in
their doctrinal and personal approaches. They place great emphasis on the centrality of Jesus Christ as the Son of the living God,
the way to God, the guide for Christian living, the source of Christian teaching, and the Savior of the world. The English Declaration
at Amsterdam (1611) describes the nature of Jesus' life and work
in terms that remain relevant to most contemporary Baptists. It
states

> that JESUS CHRIST, the Son of God the second Person, or sub-
> sistence in the Trinity, in the fullness of time was manifested in
> the Flesh, being the seed of David, and of the Israelites, accord-
> ing to the Flesh. Romans 1:3 and 8:5. [and] the Son of Mary the
> Virgin, made of her substance, Galatians 4:4. By the power of
> the HOLY GHOST overshadowing her, Luke 1:35 and being
> thus true Man was like unto us in all thing[s], sin only excepted.
> Hebrews 4:15, being one person in two distinct natures, TRUE
> GOD, and TRUE MAN. (Lumpkin, 119)

But beyond the doctrinal affirmations of who Jesus is, Baptists
run to Jesus as personal savior and eternal friend, and testify to
having had "a direct experience with Jesus Christ." This saving
event is the entry into a direct relationship with God made possible in Christ. To be Christian, therefore, is to be "born again" in
response to the love and grace revealed in Jesus Christ. Again, the
English Declaration notes

that Jesus Christ is Mediator of the New Testament between GOD and Man, I Timothy 2:5, having all power in heaven and in Earth given to him, Matthew 28:18. Being the only KING, Luke 1:33, PRIEST, Hebrews 7:24, and PROPHET, Acts 3:22. (Lumpkin, 119)

13. What does "incarnation" mean?

John's Gospel says, "The Word became flesh and dwelt among us and we beheld his glory, the glory as of the only begotten of the Father, full of grace and truth (John 1:14 KJV). "The Word became flesh": that is the beginning of incarnation. Baptists join other Christians in asserting that Jesus is the sign that God has entered human history, "taken on flesh," and become a human being. Jesus did not "seem" to be human as the Gnostics claimed. Rather, as 1 John says, he was the "Word of life," "which we have seen with our eyes, which we have looked upon, and our hands have handled" (1 John 1:1 KJV).

In the Orthodox Creed of 1678 the General Baptists stated,

We believe the person of the son of God, being a person from all eternity existing, did assume the most pure nature of man, wanting all personal existing of its own, into the unity of his person, or Godhead, and made it his own; the properties of each nature being preserved, and this inseparable and indissolvable union of both natures . . . and of two natures is one Christ, God-man, or Immanuel, God with us. (Lumpkin, 300)

Baptists believe that Jesus became a human being, bore both the divine and human in his life, and offered himself as a sacrifice for the sins of the world. This strong theological statement is restated in the popular piety of Baptist life in the simple words of Scripture: "God was in Christ reconciling the world to himself" (Col. 5:19 KJV). The incarnation not only means that God entered human history. It means he did so *for each one of us!*

14. Was Jesus born of a virgin?

Like Mary the mother of Jesus, when we confront news of the incarnation we may ask, "How can this be?" (Luke 1:34 NEB). The virgin birth is a timeless affirmation that stretches from Luke's Gospel to the present day, not without mystery and not without controversy. The earliest Baptist confessions of faith affirm the virgin birth, often with citations from Scripture. The Short Confession written in 1610 by the little band of Baptists in Amsterdam asserts that the "Word, or Son" became flesh "in the womb of the holy virgin (called Mary) by his word, and power and the working of the Holy Ghost" (Lumpkin, 104). The Somerset Confession of 1656 simply joins together segments of certain Gospel texts, noting

> That when the fullness of time was come, God sent forth his Son, made of a woman (Gal. 4:4–5) according to the promises and prophesies of the scriptures; who was conceived in the womb of Mary the virgin by the power of the Holy spirit of God, (Luke 1:35; Matt. 1:20), and by her born in Bethlehem (Matt. 2:11; Luke 2:6–7). (Lumpkin, 206)

Generally speaking, most Baptists affirm both the biological and theological uniqueness of the virgin birth of Christ. For those Baptists, the virgin birth is a biological miracle that only God could engender as a means of accomplishing the incarnation and perpetuating a sinless savior. Theologically, many Baptists insist that the virgin birth is essential to the sinless nature of the Christ, thereby making him an appropriate sacrifice for the sins of the world. It means that Jesus was conceived apart from the curse of original sin.

In the twentieth century the growth of the fundamentalist/liberal controversy made the virgin birth a matter of considerable debate among many Baptists. Fundamentalists insisted that belief in the virgin birth was one of the nonnegotiable "Five Points" of essential doctrine. Liberals suggested that the dogma was a way that prescientific Christians stressed the uniqueness of Christ's presence in the world. In his famous sermon "Shall the Fundamentalists Win?" (1922) liberal Baptist preacher Harry Emerson Fosdick observed that while "many are the gracious and beautiful souls that hold to" the idea of Christ's virgin birth, "side by side with them in the evangelical churches is a group of equally loyal and reverent people who would say that the virgin birth is not to be accepted as an historical fact."* He noted that the "two men who contributed most to the Church's thought of the divine meaning of the Christ were Paul and John, who never even distinctly allude to the virgin birth." (Smith, et al., 297). Others responded that it is quite possible that both John and Paul assumed that the virgin birth was a reality and saw no need to reference it.

Debates over the virgin birth continue among certain Baptists, although with perhaps less intensity than in the twentieth century. The overwhelming majority of Baptist church members affirm the virgin birth as a sign of Christ's unique relationship to God and humanity as well as an important biblical assertion. In the hymn "Silent Night, Holy Night" they continue to sing at Christmastime a lullaby affirmation of faith: "Round yon virgin mother and child! Holy Infant so tender and mild, sleep in heavenly peace."

15. Who is the Virgin Mary?

To say that Jesus was "born of a virgin" is to ask questions about the role of Mary the mother of Jesus in the Bible and in the church. Mary's Magnificat set forth in Luke 1:46–55 puts her center stage in that version of Jesus' birth. In the Gospels of Luke and John she and her Son have only two direct conversations, both of which are a bit edgy, to say the least. In Luke, after Jesus was nowhere to be found as the family returned from Jerusalem to

*H. E. Fosdick, "Shall the Fundamentalists Win?" in Shelton Handy, Robert T. Loetscher, and Lefferts A. Smith, eds. *American Christianity, vol. 2: 1820–1960* (New York: Charles Scribner's Sons, 1963), 297.

Nazareth, you can hear the classic parental anxiety in her voice when they finally discover him in the Temple talking to the elders. "'Child,'" she says to the Son of God, "'why have you treated us like this? Look, your father and I have been searching for you in great anxiety.'" (Luke 2:48). Then in John's Gospel, at the wedding of Cana in Galilee it is Jesus who responds with directness after she offers a one-sentence assessment of the crisis at the party: "'They have no wine.'" (John 2:3). This time it is Jesus who responds with certain directness: "'Woman,'" he says to his own mother, "'what concern is that to you and me? My hour has not yet come.'" (John 2:4). Nonetheless the Son fulfills the Mother's request. Mary is also present with the "other women" who remain at the cross, apparently after all the bona fide apostles had run for cover.

Baptists have generally acknowledged those biblical stories about Mary's presence in the early Christian communities but have often minimized her significance in part because of a desire to distance themselves from the claims of Roman Catholics regarding Mary as *theotokos* (Mother of God) or "Chief Mediatrix" (a unique role in God's plan of salvation). They also reject the idea of Mary's "perpetual virginity" (she had no other children after Jesus' birth), her Immaculate Conception (that she was herself conceived without the curse of original sin), and bodily assumption (Mary did not see death but was taken away into heaven).

More recently, perhaps as part of the women's movement in many Baptist churches, various clergy and laity have revisited the significance of Mary both in the New Testament and as the face of the feminine in Christian history. Some have even rediscovered the full text of the Magnificat, the song she sings when she learns that she is to bear a special child. Half praise chorus, half socio-economic manifesto, the Magnificat begins with a declaration of celebration and rejoicing as Mary sings,

> "Tell out, my soul, the greatness of the Lord,
> rejoice, rejoice, my spirit, in God my saviour;
> so tenderly has he looked upon his servant,
> humble as she is.

> For, from this day forth,
> all generations will count me blessed,
> so wonderfully has he dealt with me,
> the Lord, the Mighty One."
>
> (Luke 1:46–49 NEB)

But then the song turns to social commentary:

> "The arrogant of heart and mind he has put to rout,
> he has torn imperial powers from their thrones,
> but the humble have been lifted high.
> The hungry he has satisfied with good things,
> the rich sent empty away."
>
> (Luke 1:51–53 NEB)

Baptists would do well to recover Mary's "voice" as a guide for praising God and acting prophetically in the world. We neglect her witness for and with her Son at our peril.

16. Why did Jesus die on the Cross?

Most Baptists "in the pew" would probably answer this question by insisting that Jesus had to die on the cross as God's chosen instrument as one who "takes away the sins of the world" (John 1:29). They would acknowledge that while Jesus prayed agonizingly in the Garden of Gethsemane that the "cup" of suffering be taken away from him, he acquiesced, "'Yet not what I will, but what thou wilt'" (Mark 14:35–36 NEB).

Theological debates continue as to whether Jesus was God's intended "victim" from the beginning of time, whether he chose to sacrifice himself, or whether he responded courageously and sacrificially to circumstances that were thrust upon him.

Baptist confessions of faith offer varying statements on the meaning of Jesus' death on the cross. One of the earliest, the Short Confession of 1610, points to Jesus' work as "High Priest and Mediator" as evidenced in the fact that "he hath finally given himself obediently (for the reconciliation of the sins of the world) to all outward suffering, and hath offered up himself in death upon the cross unto the Father, for a sweet savor and common oblation" (Lumpkin, 105–6). (Oblation is a gift offered to a deity.) The Standard Confession of General Baptists (1660) uses language taken from Scripture to assert that Christ "freely gave himself a ransom for all, I Timothy 2:5–6, tasting death for every man, Hebrews 2:9, a propitiation for our sins; and not for ours only, but also for the sins of the whole World, I John 2:2" (Lumpkin, 225). The Orthodox Creed (1678) goes into greater detail as to the work of Christ on the cross and notes that Jesus, "by the sacrifice of himself, which he, thro' the eternal spirit offered up unto the father, hath fully satisfied the justice of God and reconciled him to us." It also makes clear that "God the father . . . did chuse [sic] Jesus Christ, and sent him into the world to die for Adam, or fallen man" (Lumpkin, 310).

These statements reflect varying Baptist interpretations of the atonement, the restoration of fallen humanity's relationship with God. Theological options for explaining the atonement include the "ransom theory" that Christ's death was a ransom paid to the devil to purchase human redemption and the "substitutionary or sacrificial theory" that Christ's death was offered to a righteous God for the sins of the species. That is, Christ was the sinless substitute who took upon himself the punishment required of humanity by God's justice. Another atonement theory involves the "moral influence theory" that Christ's life and death illustrate the lengths to which God goes to set a new example for restoring lost relationship with God. Those who follow Christ are thus empowered to live as Jesus lived in fellowship with God. Still another theory suggests that Christ's death proves that he is the ultimate "victor" over sin and death.

These days, conservative Baptists tend toward the substitutionary theory of the atonement, many insisting that it is one of the nonnegotiable fundamentals of the faith. Others gravitate toward the moral influence or "Christus Victor" approaches to the atonement that suggest Christ's example of total faithfulness to God or his ultimate triumph over death and evil. Debates over the orthodoxy of one or the other approaches continue unabated in many quarters of Baptist life. All would generally agree, however, that Christ's death on the cross accomplished something unique in restoring fallen humanity to a new relationship with God. Amid theological debates, surely Baptists can sing out the words in the hymn "When I Survey the Wondrous Cross," together,

> Were the whole realm of nature mine,
> That were a present far too small.
> Love so amazing, so Divine,
> Demands my soul, my life, my all.

17. What is the meaning of the resurrection of Jesus Christ?

At first glance it is easy to say that Baptists, like other Christians worldwide, are deeply committed to a belief in the resurrection of Jesus Christ. All the early Baptist confessions give attention to that signal event as essential to understanding the nature and veracity of the church's claims as a New Community. The Short Confession (1610) says it eloquently:

> Having accomplished and performed here upon the earth, by dying the death, his office of the cross he was afterwards buried, thereby declaring that he was truly dead; the third day he rose again, and stood up from the dead, abolishing death, and testifying that he was Lord over death, and he could not possibly be detained by the hands of death, thereby comfortably assuring all the faithful of their resurrection and standing up from death. (Lumpkin, 106)

What a wonderful phrase: "comfortably assuring" the "faithful of their resurrection!"

Yet in spite of the centuries of the church's affirmation of Christ's resurrection, Baptists also recognize that it is no easy affirmation in the twenty-first century any more than it was in the first century. To read the honest accounts of the Gospels, belief in the resurrection proved quite difficult, even for the people who experienced it "upfront and personal." Indeed, while Thomas the apostle carries the label "doubter" across the church's history, doubting was apparently true of all the male followers of Jesus, for Luke says that when the *women* told them the news, "the story appeared to them to be *nonsense,* and they would not believe them" (Luke 24:10–11 NEB, italics added). Even when Jesus showed up and was "standing among them," they "thought they were seeing a ghost," and "were still unconvinced, still wondering, for *it seemed too good to be true*" (Luke 24: 41 NEB, italics added). Finally, John's Gospel sorts out the doubt then and now as Jesus reveals himself to Thomas, who touches Christ's hands and side and believes, only to have the Master remind him (and us), "'Because you have seen me you have found faith. Happy are they who *never saw me and yet have found faith'*" (John 20:29 NEB, italics added).

Generally speaking, seventeenth-century Baptist confessions of faith readily affirm the resurrection of Christ but seem to give more specific attention to Christ's death on the cross. (I'm generalizing here.) It is in certain statements on baptismal immersion that they implicitly remind the faithful that this sacrament/ordinance is the believer's way of identifying with Christ in death and resurrection. The Orthodox Creed declares that baptism is "to be unto the party baptized, or dipped, a sign of our entrance into the covenant of grace, and ingrafting into Christ, and into the body of Christ, . . . and our fellowship with Christ, *in his death and resurrection,* and of our living, or rising to newness of life" (Lumpkin, 317).

Baptist piety also suggests that Christ's work on the cross is not some legal transaction but a human engagement of sin and suffering, not only for itself but for the "sins of the world." Jesus, the dying and rising savior, is therefore the gentle friend who draws near to us with the greatest Christian graces, modeling the dramatic nature of servanthood in his life, work, and preaching.

It remains for a later document, the New Hampshire Confession (1833), to set forth a rather simple and sweet statement acknowledging Christ's "personal obedience" and "atonement for our sins by his death; being risen from the dead he is now enthroned in heaven; and uniting in his wonderful person the tenderest sympathies with divine perfections, [he] is ever qualified to be a suitable, a compassionate, and an all-sufficient Saviour" (Lumpkin, 362–63). Very suitable indeed.

18. Will there be a second coming of Jesus Christ?

Christians have anticipated the return of Christ since the book of Thessalonians appeared in 45 AD:

> For this we tell you as the Lord's word: we who are left alive until the Lord comes shall not forestall those who have died; because at the word of command, at the sound of the archangel's voice and God's trumpet-call, the Lord himself will descend from heaven; first the Christian dead will rise, then we who are left alive shall join them, caught up in clouds to meet the Lord in the air. Thus we shall always be with the Lord. (1 Thess. 4:15–17 NEB)

Theories of eschatology (last things) abound in the church and cover a wide spectrum of ideas regarding the specifics of Christ's return. Many revolve around the idea of a millennium, that thousand-year period spoken of in the twentieth chapter of the book of Revelation and discussed elsewhere in this volume. Suffice it to say that while Baptists disagree over many of the details of Christ's return, they believe that it will happen: the faithful will be "saved," evil will be defeated, and a new heaven and new earth will take shape through the power of God.

Seventeenth-century Baptist confessions of faith often (but not always) address "last things" and the judgment that is to come at the "end time." The Somerset Confession (1656) offers a concise statement that reflects the directions of other such documents. It reads,

> It is our assured expectation, grounded upon promises, that the Lord Jesus Christ shall the second time appear without sin unto salvation, unto his people, to raise and change the vile bodies of all his saints, to fashion them like unto his glorious body, and so to reign with him, and judge over all nations on the earth in power and glory. (Lumpkin, 214)

4

Holy Spirit

19. How do we understand the nature of the Holy Spirit?

The Apostles' Creed begins, "I believe in God the Father Almighty, maker of heaven and earth, and in Jesus Christ, his only Son our Lord." It then elaborates a bit on basic elements in the life and work of Jesus. Next, almost as an afterthought it adds, "I believe in the Holy Spirit." Enough said?

In essence, the Holy Spirit is the continuing, unseen presence of God in the world. In a sense Spirit-language begins with Genesis and the statement that "the spirit of God [in Hebrew the word is *ruach*] hovered over the surface of the waters" (Gen. 1:2 REB). Jesus predicts the coming of that presence he calls the "Advocate" or "Comforter," who will teach his followers "everything" (John 14:25–26 REB). In John's Gospel the resurrected Christ "breathes on" the fearful apostolic community and says, "Receive the Holy Spirit" (John 20:22).

And then there is Pentecost, the classic moment in Christian history when the Spirit descended on the fledgling band of disciples with power that appeared like "tongues of fire" (Acts 2:3 REB) and enabled them to speak in the various languages of people gathered for the Jewish feast. Pentecost represents the coming of the Holy Spirit into the Church and the world with power (Acts 2:1–13).

Later Christians debated the source of the Spirit, a difference of opinion that continues to exist in various churches. By the sixth century, Christians in the West began to extend the Nicene Creed to say that the Spirit "proceeds from the Father and the Son," with the latter phrase translated as *filioque* ("from the Son") in Latin. Eastern Orthodox Christians reject that statement, insisting that such a statement was a heretical addition to the creed. The Nicene Creed, using *filioque,* continues to be used in Roman Catholic and Protestant churches but not in Eastern Orthodox communions.

Baptist confessions of faith, like other documents of the church, refer primarily to the Holy Spirit as the third "person" of the Trinity. In fact, most of the confessions give limited attention to the nature of the Holy Spirit. The Orthodox Creed of 1678 has one of the most extensive statements on the Holy Spirit of any of the Baptist confessions. It states,

> We believe that there is one holy spirit, the third person subsisting in the sacred trinity, one with the father and son, who is very and true God, of one substance or nature with the father and son, coequal, coeternal, and coessential with the father and son, to whom with the father and son, three persons, and but one eternal and almighty God, be by all the hosts of saints and angels, ascribed eternal glory, and Hallelujahs. Amen. (Lumpkin, 301)

20. How does the Holy Spirit come to us?

Among Christians in general and Protestants in particular there are a variety of opinions on how persons receive the Holy Spirit. Some view the Spirit's presence as the "Hound of Heaven," following persons throughout their lives, nudging them through experience and circumstance to receive the gifts of God's grace. Some believe that the Spirit comes upon persons in the great sacraments of the church—baptism, confirmation, Communion, life vocation, confession of sin, and preparation for death. Some suggest that the Spirit in its fullness comes in conversion and baptism, recognized and chosen by sinners who accept and live "in Christ." Some suggest that the fullness of God's presence is known in the "baptism of the Holy Spirit" received for sanctification (holiness of life) as evidenced in healing and glossolalia (speaking in tongues). Whatever the specific theology of the Spirit, however, all would agree that the Holy Spirit is essential for the Christian disciple, recognized or not.

As conversionists, committed to the idea of a believers' church, Baptists have generally asserted that the Holy Spirit is the agent of salvation and regeneration (new life) experienced in conversion and represented in the sacrament/ordinance of baptism. The General Baptist confession, known as "The True Gospel Faith Declared According to the Scriptures" (1654) states simply, "They that believe the things so preached ought to be dipped in water, Acts 10:47. Can any man forbid water that these should not be baptized [which in English is "Dipped"] which have received the Holy Spirit as well as we?" It concludes, "God gives his Spirit to believers dipped through the prayer of faith and laying on of hands, Acts 8:15; Acts 8:17; Acts 5:32; Ephes. 1:13–14" (Lumpkin, 193).

The baptism of the Holy Spirit thus accompanied baptism itself. Those who confess Christ in baptism receive it "in the name of the Father, and of the Son, *and of the Holy Spirit*" (italics added). Likewise, the confession notes that the power to extend the Gospel is made possible through the gift of the Spirit, as it says, "[God] hath given down the holy spirit to his Servants, that they might make known to all Nations the things that concern the Name of Jesus and the Kingdom of Heaven" (Lumpkin, 193).

While some Baptists do claim the baptism of the Holy Spirit as a second gift of grace, most continue to believe, implicitly or explicitly, that the Spirit is the agent of conversion, coming in fullness when we "receive Christ" as savior and experience baptism into Christ's body, the church. Through the power of the Spirit, cultivated in a life of Christian discipleship, the individual grows in God's grace.

21. What is the baptism of the Holy Spirit?

The phrase "baptism of the Holy Spirit" has become increasingly important (and controversial) as the pentecostal and charismatic movements have expanded across the world. While the concept has no specific reference in the New Testament, it grows out of Jesus' description in the Gospels (such as Mark 1:8 REB), that "the one who is to come . . . will baptize you with the Holy Spirit." Its roots lie with the division among certain Protestants between justification (entering into faith) and sanctification (going on in grace). These distinctions were a common theme in the sermons of John Wesley, the founder of Methodism, and in certain denominations such as the Church of the Nazarene. The Holy Spirit is thus the agent of sanctification or holiness that is required of all true believers who would be followers of Christ. Holiness churches in the Wesleyan tradition spoke of Spirit baptism as the sign of and empowerment for holiness and the "deeper Christian life." By 1906 one segment of the holiness movement became the pentecostal movement, with its belief that the gifts of the early church's pentecostal experience had been repeated in the present. Thus the baptism of the Holy Spirit with signs of healing and speaking in tongues became the hallmark of a new Christian community. In some cases the experience of tongues is given only to the individual, with no "translation" for the community of faith. At other times, Pentecostals believe that the tongues may be "interpreted" for the church by other persons present in the worshiping congregation.

More recently, the charismatic movement continued an earlier emphasis on the gifts of the Spirit, especially evident in the personal spirituality of the Christian. Yet these charismatic experiences born of the Spirit need not include actual speaking in tongues. Some persons who consider themselves charismatic often testify to speaking in tongues, but only as private "prayer language" carried out in personal devotions, not in public worship.

None of the seventeenth-century Baptist confessions of faith use that phrase in any of their theological statements. In fact, most early Baptists would have agreed with their Reformed counterparts that justification and sanctification were simultaneously bestowed in the redemptive process. Some even suggest that the pentecostal gifts—tongues, healing, prophecy—were a "one time outpouring" that cannot be repeated. The Holy Spirit, essential for conversion, immediately brought sanctification to the new believer. The sign of this double blessing was immersion baptism. The Orthodox Creed of General Baptists states,

> Those that are united unto Christ by effectual faith, are regenerated, and have a new heart and spirit created in them through the virtue of Christ, his death, resurrection, and intercession, and by efficacy of the holy spirit, received by faith, and are sanctified by the word and spirit of truth, dwelling in them. (Lumpkin, 316)

22. What is the work of the Holy Spirit?

Christians believe that the Holy Spirit is not a separate deity but the Spirit of God, present in the church and the world. Its work includes the following:

1. The Spirit *inspires* persons to speak and act in the world. Jesus told his disciples, "But when you are arrested, do not worry about what you are to say; when the time comes, the words you need will be given you; for it is not you who are speaking: it will be the Spirit of your Father speaking in you" (Matt. 10:19–20 NEB).
2. The Spirit brings *callings* for ministry in the church and the world. St. Paul says these "gifts" of calling include "some to be apostles, some prophets, some evangelists, some pastors and teachers, to equip God's people for work in his service, to the building up of the body of Christ. (Eph. 4:11–12 NEB).
3. The Spirit bestows *spiritual gifts* for living. These are the *charismata* (gifts) of the Spirit that include "love, joy, peace, patience, kindness, goodness, fidelity, gentleness, and self-control (Gal. 5:22–23 NEB).
4. The Spirit is the agent of both *justification and sanctification* in the process of faith.

The New Hampshire Confession says that "sanctification is the process by which . . . we are made partakers of [God's] holiness; that it is a progressive work; that it is begun in regeneration; and that it is carried on in the hearts of believers by the presence and power of the Holy Spirit" (Lumpkin, 365).

The Holy Spirit also is at work in the world; it is the stealth presence of God moving in places and persons that often the world (and the church) do not recognize immediately, if ever. Augustine's famous work *Confessions* testifies to the fact that even when we do not recognize it, the Spirit is present. Only when we look back on life with eyes of faith do we see the presence of the Spirit at moments unacknowledged and unknown when they actually occurred. The Spirit blows where it will, and we do not know where it begins or ends. It is the eternal mystery with us and beyond us, God's unseen presence in the world. With all these good gifts the church's continuing prayer should be "Come, Holy Spirit."

5

Humanity

23. What is the nature of the human condition?

For most Baptists, like many other Christians, the Augustinian vision of the human condition is perhaps the most widely known and accepted approach to understanding what it means to be human. The early Baptist confessions of faith, both Arminian and Calvinist, reflect that traditional understanding of the nature of the fall of Adam and Eve, the introduction of human sin, and the process of human redemption. The Short Confession (1610) written by the Baptists in Amsterdam lays out the story with clarity, noting, "This only God hath created man good, according to his image and likeness, to a good and happy estate, and in him all men to the same blessed end" (Lumpkin, 103). Thus the original intent of the Creator was that human beings reflect goodness and happiness, a state befitting those who are made in the divine image. However, as the English Declaration (1611) asserts,

> This GOD in the beginning created all things of nothing, Gen. 1:1, and made man of the dust of the earth, Gen. 2:7, in his own image, Gen. 1:27, in righteousness and true Holiness, Ephes. 4:24: yet being tempted, fell by disobedience, Gen. 3:1–7. Through whose disobedience, all men sinned, Rom. 5:12–19. His sin being imputed unto all; and so death went over all men. (Lumpkin, 117)

Thus this confession concludes, "That notwithstanding this Men are by nature the Children of wrath, Ephes. 2:3, born in iniquity and in sin conceived" (Lumpkin, 117).

Baptists generally suggest that the human condition is one of mixed realities. On one hand, all persons are created in the image of God (*imago dei*) for communion and relationship with the Creator. On the other, an inherent sinfulness has descended on our species, disrupting that fellowship. Some tend to place more emphasis on the image of God in humanity while others stress the total sinfulness of the human creature. The remedy for restoration of fellowship is through faith in Jesus Christ. Many Baptists would agree with Irenaeus, the second-century theologian who wrote that Christ "recapitulated [summed up] in himself the long line of the human race, procuring for us salvation thus summarily, so that what we had lost in Adam, that is, the being in the image and likeness of God, that we should regain in Christ Jesus" (Bettenson, 30).

24. What do we mean by "original" sin?

I once had a professor who approached the topic of original sin by asking his students to produce one! He then told us that he sincerely doubted that possibility since all the sins he knew about had no doubt been attempted long before any of us arrived on the scene. He did allow, however, that it might be possible to accomplish a truly original sin, for human beings are a decidedly intelligent and creative species!

The idea or doctrine of original sin is essentially an issue of beginnings. It offers a response to the question of how it is that human beings can be capable of so much good and so much evil, with a strong emphasis on the reality of evil in the world. It is one small effort to respond to those innumerable atrocities evident in the Inquisition, the Middle Passage (slave trade), and the Holocaust (among other horrors of human initiative) that illustrate the depth of evil in the world. The Hebrew description of the "fall" of Adam and Eve in the garden, as articulated and expanded by Christian interpreters, is perhaps the most widely known and (to varying degrees) widely accepted notion of original sin across the history of the church. In this story, the primeval couple, Adam and

Eve, as described in Gen. 1–3, are created by God, placed in a wonderful garden, and given great power and freedom within the overall creation (the power of naming, for example). They violate the divine command, try to cover up their sin, and are then banished forever from the garden. As the Confession of Faith and Ecclesiastical Principles of the Evangelical Association of French-speaking Baptist Churches (1879, 1924) says,

> We believe that our first parents were created innocent, but having willfully disobeyed their creator, they lost their primitive estate and incurred the just judgment of God. All their descendants enveloped in this judgment and inheriting their fallen nature are inclined towards evil. (Lumpkin, 412)

Christian theologians such as Augustine and Calvin, reading those Hebrew texts, concluded that the sin of Adam and Eve was passed on spiritually, if not biologically, to the entire human species. It remains inside the theological DNA of every person born into the world. Augustine (d. 410), writing in the fourth century, concluded that the evidence of this sin was "concupiscence," a corruption of the will, evident in the human desire "to have it all" apart from any recognition of the Creator. Augustine did not believe that original sin was passed on through sexual intercourse but that the defilement of sexual purity by improper desire, even in marriage, was evidence of that corruption. Children therefore entered the world with the curse of sin already upon them, and immediate baptism for infants was necessary to cleanse them from such a condition.

If Baptists agree that the human species is "fallen," they do not necessarily agree on the results of the fall. While generally accepting Augustine's diagnosis, they rejected his cure, rejecting the baptism of infants and deferring it until faith can be chosen and testified to by the individual (adult) believer. Arminian Baptists argue, as the English Declaration suggests, that, "now being fallen, and having all disposition unto evil, and no disposition or will unto any good, yet GOD giving grace, man may receive grace, or may reject grace" (Lumpkin, 117–18). From this perspective, human beings, though evil, still have the power to accept or reject God's grace. John Smyth's Short Confession (1610) is amazing in its directness. It states, "There is no original sin, [lit. *no sin of origin or descent*], but all sin is actual and voluntary, viz. a word, a deed, or a design against the law of God; and therefore, infants are without sin" (Lumpkin, 100).

Smyth made the choice of sin a free response of each individual born into the world, not the responsibility of the first "parents." His position was also a response to infant baptism (denying its necessity and validity) by those who believed that baptism should be given only to adult believers. In a parallel Short Confession the Baptists in Amsterdam asserted, "The causes and ground . . . of man's destruction and damnation, are the man's free choice of darkness or sin, and living therein. Destruction, therefore cometh out of [human beings], but not from the good Creator" (Lumpkin, 104).

Those of more Calvinist sentiments limit those choices, as noted in the First London Confession (1644): "And touching his creature man, God had in Christ before the foundation of the world, according to the good pleasure of his will, foreordained *some men* to eternal life through Jesus Christ, to the praise and glory of his grace, leaving the rest in their sin to their just condemnation, to the praise of his Justice" (Lumpkin, 157, italics added). For these Baptists, only the elect have the opportunity to affect their "natural state" of sinfulness. All others cannot receive grace and must live out their condemned condition.

Later Baptists often challenged the idea of inherent human corruption, suggesting a more optimistic view. While human sin was clearly present, it was not the result of some ancient curse based on biology but on the long history of sinful behavior in the lives of human beings. For some Baptists, the question of original sin and original grace begins anew with each new life, not with long-absent spiritual parents.

Amid these divisions, the centrality of Jesus Christ as the one who restores what humanity lost, past and present, personal and social, is of major importance for the church.

25. Do human beings really have free will?

Of course we do. But how we get it, where it takes us, and what it means to our spirituality are matters of serious debate in the church in general and among Baptists in particular! Early Baptist confessions seldom if ever use the phrase "free will," yet they clearly distinguish differences of opinion as to when persons are able to exercise certain freedom of choice in a spiritual response to grace. Essentially, Calvinists believe that human beings are so totally depraved that they have no free will whereby to choose grace until it is "infused" into the heart of the elect from God alone. The Midland Confession, a Particular Baptist confession of 1655, says very directly that all persons "until they be quickened by Christ are dead in trespasses—Ephesians 2:1; and therefore have no power of themselves to believe savingly—John 15:5" (Lumpkin, 199). Thus, there is no free will until God gives it to the elect. The Second London Confession (1688) echoes that idea and adds that only "when God converts a sinner, and translates him into the state of Grace, he freeth him from his natural bondage under sin, and by his grace alone, enables him freely to will, and to do that which is spiritually good" (Lumpkin, 264).

General (Arminian) Baptists see free will very differently, believing that there remains, even after the fall, a modicum of "enabling grace" (sometimes known as prevenient grace) that permits sinners to choose grace. Free will "enables" sinners to reach toward God's saving grace, which is reaching toward sinners. Thus free will is a genuine element of the process of salvation. As the General Baptists suggest in their Faith and Practise of Thirty Congregations (1651), "Those gifts which God of his free grace gives unto men to the enabling or empowering them to obey or believe in his name, are called the grace of God, as they spring from the spirit of grace; Acts 18:17" (Lumpkin, 179–80).

John Smyth's Short Confession is clear that because of "the grace of God through the redemption of Christ," all human beings "are able (the Holy Spirit, by grace, being before unto them *grace prevemènt)* [prevenient grace] to repent, to believe, to turn to God, and to attain to eternal life; so on the other hand, they are able themselves to resist the Holy Spirit, to depart from God, and to perish for ever" (Lumpkin, 100–101). Human free will (enabling grace) cooperates with God's saving grace to accomplish salvation. Likewise, if one has the free will to accept Christ, one also has the free will to reject Christ along the way.

The New Hampshire Confession (1833) splits the difference between Arminian and Calvinist for a more "blended" theological view in its suggestion that "election is the gracious purpose of God, according to which he [graciously] regenerates, sanctifies, and saves sinners; that being perfectly consistent with the *free agency of man,* it comprehends all the means in connection with the end" (Lumpkin, 364, italics added). In other words, by 1833 some Baptists were trying to reconcile election and free will, a fascinating effort to solve an ancient theological dilemma.

Whatever else we may say, the freedom to choose is closely related to Baptist understanding of the nature of the human conscience, whether individuals have professed Christian faith or not.

26. What is the nature of the human conscience?

Many of the early Baptist confessions of faith emphasize the role of conscience as an identifying mark of humanity, a trait that distinguishes them from other mammals. It offers a valuable insight not only to the beginnings of the tradition but also for present issues related to the nature of the human condition. For many Baptists, the existence of conscience made each individual responsible to God alone for decisions related to faith or nonfaith, good and evil, freedom and responsibility. Conscience is at once a kind of moral compass that helps us sort out right from wrong and at its best is an internal warning signal when we step over ethical boundaries. Conscience is our inner "governor" that alarms us when we are or are considering acting inappropriately.

Yet for early Baptists conscience is also the door to human freedom, the opportunity for every person to exercise a choice to accept or reject relationship with God. And only God can judge the human conscience in matters of faith and religious life. Likewise, those who do choose faith are bound by conscience to oppose all those actions of state or culture that contradict or challenge the inner code of spirituality and ethics. Many Baptists went to prison or faced exile in seventeenth-century England and America as a "matter of conscience" rather than violate religious convictions. The Second London Confession makes clear that "God alone is Lord of the conscience, and hath left it free from the Doctrines and Commandments of men which are in any thing contrary to his Word" (Lumpkin, 279–80). For Baptists conscience is real, conscience is judged only by God, and conscience is the foundation of religious liberty and uncoerced faith.

6

Salvation

27. What is the process of salvation?

Baptists speak extensively about the need to be "saved" from sin to a new life in Jesus Christ. Indeed, the Baptist movement began with the insistence of the earliest communities that the church was to be composed only of those who could claim an experience of salvation. The foundational principle of a "believers' church" is built on the idea that all members can testify to an experience of grace in their hearts. When Baptists refer to salvation they use such terms as conversion, being born again, a personal experience with Christ, or new life in Christ.

Thus the process of salvation is essential to Baptist identity. First, the process of salvation begins with God, not with human beings. God is the author of salvation, from creation to the death and resurrection of Jesus Christ. God makes salvation happen. Second, salvation is uncoerced. Each individual is responsible for his or her response to the grace of God made known in Jesus Christ. Third, salvation finds different people in a variety of ways, so surefire methods are elusive at best, confusing at worst. Some persons are nurtured into faith gradually, perhaps from childhood, in more subtle ways. Such individuals often say that they grew up in the faith and never knew a time when they did not know and love Jesus. Others, perhaps blind to the possibilities for or need of grace at certain points in life, come to faith after great trauma or in a momentous experience. Others may share elements of both journeys toward faith.

Fourth, salvation involves repentance from sin and faith in Jesus Christ, a turning from one way of looking at life to another. Fifth, salvation is not simply a one-time act, but a lifelong journey of growing in grace. The New Hampshire Confession (1833) states

> that in order to be saved, we must be regenerated or born again; that regeneration consists in giving a holy disposition to the mind; and is effected in a manner above our comprehension or calculation by the power of the Holy Spirit, . . . so as to secure our voluntary obedience to the Gospel; and that its proper evidence is found in the holy fruit which we bring forth to the glory of God. (Lumpkin, 364)

These general characteristics are acceptable to most Baptists who delineate the steps to salvation. Disagreements remain, especially as related to the proper candidates for conversion, the nature of election, and the way in which regeneration (new birth) occurs. Arminian-related Baptists insist, as noted earlier, that all human beings are potentially elected to salvation, but only those who come on the terms of election—repentance and faith—are actually elected. The English Declaration of 1611 says that God "before the foundation of the world . . . predestinated that all that believe in him shall be saved" (Lumpkin, 118). Thus all persons are potentially elected to salvation but are actually elected only after freely choosing to repent and believe the Gospel. Salvation, or the lack thereof, is the responsibility of every living person (Lumpkin, 117–18).

Human free will (enabling grace) cooperates with God's saving grace to accomplish salvation. Likewise, if one has the free will to accept Christ, one also has the free will to reject Christ along the way. The English Declaration acknowledges that humans

> may fall away from the grace of GOD, Heb. 12:15 and from the truth, which they have received & acknowledged, Heb. 10:26 after they have tasted of the heavenly gift, and were made partakers of the HOLY GHOST, and have tasted of the good word of GOD, and of the powers of the world to come. (Lumpkin, 118)

Salvation, once claimed, can be intentionally deserted; falling from grace is a real possibility.

Calvinist Baptists, however, view the boundaries of salvation very differently, insisting that the human race is a *massa damnata* (a damned mass) incapable of exercising free will or choosing anything but evil. Even the good works of the totally depraved are tainted by impure, sinful motives. The Articles of Faith of the Kehukee Primitive Baptist Association (1827) in North Carolina says plainly that "it is utterly out of the power of men, as fallen creatures, to keep the law of God perfectly, repent of their sins truly, or believe in Jesus Christ, except they be drawn by the Holy Ghost" (Lumpkin, 355). Since everyone deserves salvation, it is a gift of grace that God should save any. Thus God unconditionally chose some persons for salvation before the foundation of the world. The First London Confession (1644) says it clearly: "Christ Jesus by his death did bring forth salvation and reconciliation only for the elect, which were those which God the Father gave him & and . . . the Gospel which is to be preached to all men as the ground of faith" (Lumpkin, 162).

Calvinist Baptists believe that salvation is based on God's sovereign and merciful choice of some persons unconditionally. There is nothing sinners can do to justify that election in themselves. Grace will find those elect individuals before they leave this world. And whom grace calls, grace keeps; the elect will persevere until the end. Again the First London Confession notes that "faith is the gift of God wrought in the hearts of the elect by the Spirit of God, whereby they come to see, know, and believe the truth of the Scriptures" (Lumpkin, 163). Those who have received this "precious faith . . . can never finally nor totally fall away" even "though many storms and floods do arise and beat against them" (Lumpkin, 163).

Primitive Baptists are especially clear that conversion must be left to God and not hurried along. The idea that one can say a prayer and "invite Jesus into your heart" is essentially a form of works righteousness, the effort of the creature to do what only God can do—provide genuine salvation. Likewise, any missionary or evangelistic activities, such as Sunday schools, sending out missionaries, or direct "witnessing" to sinners, is also a form of works righteousness to be rejected by the church. As the Second London Confession asserts, all the elect are "regenerated and saved by Christ through the Spirit; who worketh when, and where, and how he pleaseth: so also are all other elect persons, who are uncapable of being outwardly called by the Ministry of the Word" (Lumpkin,

265). Thus all the elect will be saved in Christ even if they are not called through the preaching of the church.

These processes of salvation are quite distinct. Arminian Baptists believe that repentance and faith precede regeneration and are the terms necessary to accomplish the new birth. Calvinist Baptists believe that regeneration at God's initiative must occur before the sinner can even have the free will to repent and believe. Some Baptists believe that an immediate "prayer of faith" will bring about salvation when we ask Christ to "come into our hearts," forgive our sins, and claim us as his own. Others believe that genuine conversion requires "waiting" on God's time to receive grace, a process that may take a significant period of time. But the need for salvation and an explicit profession of faith is essential for understanding the nature of Baptist identity.

28. What is the result of salvation?

Salvation, "being in Christ," is a gift of grace for the believing human being. It involves several spiritual realities:

1. Salvation is an entrance into Christ. It is to become a "new creation in Christ Jesus."
2. Salvation is a turning from sin and an experience of forgiveness made known by the undeserved grace of God.
3. Salvation involves a "new birth" into a new family, the church. All who are in Christ are part of the body of Christ, the communion of saints. While the eternal church may be a triumphant community, in its universal, this-worldly expression it is multiracial, multiethnic, global, unruly, and often irreconcilable.
4. Salvation offers the strength to live out the teachings of Jesus in the world. It offers a way of living that mirrors the life, mission, and gospel of Jesus Christ. It makes the "gifts of the Spirit" a possibility in the life of the Christian disciple.
5. Salvation offers the hope (assurance) of eternal life and the promise of the fullness of the kingdom of God. In that communion, justice, reconciliation, peace, and wholeness may be known in the fullness of God's presence.

29. What is the meaning of "Once saved, always saved"?

The phrase "Once saved, always saved" is a common affirmation among many Baptists, a way of describing the enduring power of salvation. In some sense it may be thought to be a popular way of explaining the "perseverance of the saints," the belief that grace keeps those who are elected to salvation. It is a way of saying that the redeemed cannot "fall from grace" or "lose their salvation." Concerning perseverance, the Orthodox Creed states, "Those that are effectually called, according to God's eternal purpose, being justified by faith do receive such a measure of the holy unction, from the holy spirit, by which they shall certainly persevere unto eternal life" (Lumpkin, 324).

Perseverance, however, means a continuation of Christian devotion that extends across the years and lives of those who confess faith in Christ. "Once saved, always saved" may be another way of explaining perseverance. On the other hand it has sometimes been used in ways that place more emphasis on entering into faith rather than going on in grace. It could be misunderstood to suggest that the entry to faith and the end of faith are all that matters, rather than the life of faith that shapes the life of discipleship to the end. Such a misreading may lead persons to neglect the enduring life of faith for a "quick fix" that is less about endurance than about gaining the required experience. Christians must take care that a statement intended for assurance not become a vehicle of cheap grace. Theologically speaking, justification—entering into faith—must accompany sanctification—going on in grace—in the daily life of faith. The First London Confession speaks clearly to the continuing experience of grace, noting "that the same power that converts to faith in Christ, the same power carries on the soul still through all duties, temptations, conflicts, sufferings, and continually what ever a Christian is, he is by grace, and by a constant renewed operation from God" (Lumpkin, 163).

30. What does it mean to repent?

Repentance is an important element of the salvation process. It is the heart of the turning a sinner makes from one way of life to another. The Second London Confession calls repentance "an evangelical Grace," by which an individual

> made sensible [by the Holy Spirit] of the manifold evils of his sin, doth, by Faith in Christ, humble himself for it, with godly sorrow, detestation of it, and self-abhorrency, praying for pardon, and strength of grace . . . to walk before God unto all well pleasing in all things. (Lumpkin, 270)

This statement lists some of the basic elements of repentance, including recognition of sin, humbling oneself through a process of sorrow, and disgust with sin and *with the self.* Repentance is the recognition that the creature cannot save itself but requires the interaction of divine grace, *and is willing to change* in order to attain that kind of life.

Again, repentance is not a once-for-all event that covers every sin, past, present, and future, but is instead a lifelong event. Second London adds that repentance "is to be continued through the whole course of our lives upon the account of the body of death, and the motions thereof; so it is every [one's] duty, to repent of his particular known sins, particularly" (Lumpkin, 270).

Repentance involves a sorrow for sin, a desire to relinquish and turn from sinful behavior, and the recognition that we cannot save ourselves and are ever in need of God's grace.

31. Can a Christian backslide?

Backsliding is the popular term for the practice of turning away from faith and Christian living after one has begun the journey. Here Baptists are quite divided. Calvinist/Reformed Baptists would insist that while professing Christians can from time to time fail to live up to their "effectual calling" in Christ, the perseverance of the saints means that they cannot backslide permanently and thereby abandon salvation of their own free will. Indeed, without grace they would surely abandon any semblance of faithful service. The truly elect simply cannot backslide in any extended way. Arminian/Free Will Baptists disagree and insist that while some types of backsliding can be temporary, a more serious type of backsliding can turn to apostasy (deserting the faith). In this scenario, persons choose intentionally to turn their back on the faith they once claimed. The English Declaration at Amsterdam is clear in its assertion that even after persons

> have escaped from the filthiness of the World, [they] may be tangled again therein & overcome, 2 Peter 2:20 . . . A righteous man may forsake his righteousness and perish, Ezekiel 18:24–26. And therefore let no man presume to think that because he hath, or had once grace, therefore he shall always have grace. But let all men have assurance, that if they continue unto the end, they shall be saved. (Lumpkin 118–19)

Some Baptists would suggest that a severe case of backsliding in the life of one who claims to be a Christian may actually be an indication that the person was never really converted. Those who claim conversion but cannot live according to the "narrow way" or the "hard sayings" of Jesus many never have experienced faith at all.

32. How do you actually know that you are "saved"?

One of the great questions confronting many Christians concerns the actual knowledge that salvation has been secured and that the sinner has actually passed from death to new life. In certain Christian traditions those concerns are answered by the spiritual journey offered through the sacramental life of the church. In those traditions—Roman Catholic, Lutheran, Anglican, for example—it is less a question of "Am I saved?" than of "Am I *being* saved"? Faith is nurtured through the spirituality of Word and sacrament offered in the liturgical life of the believing community.

For many evangelical Christians, specifically Baptists, the individualism inherent in the idea of a personal experience with Jesus Christ, especially when it is punctuated with the need for a transforming, "born again" conversion event, opens the door to doubts. For example, Baptist adolescents or adults may look back on their childhood conversion and wonder if they "understood enough" or were "sincere enough" or "repentant enough" to have secured a valid experience of grace. Indeed, in some Baptist circles, multiple conversions and rebaptisms occur as people reject the validity of earlier claims to salvation and seek to "settle it once and for all" that they are on the road to salvation.

In this dilemma of doubt, both Scripture and history may be helpful. As a doubtful and guilt-ridden Martin Luther said in the early 1500s, "The just shall live by *faith*" (Rom. 1:17).* Salvation is not based on our "understanding" but on God's grace through faith. Doubts, temptations, and difficulties come to all of us, but God is ever faithful. The First London Confession (1644) says it rather eloquently:

> That all believers in the time of this life, are in a continual warfare, and opposition against sin, self, the world, and the Devil, and liable to all manner of afflictions, tribulations, and persecutions, and so shall continue until Christ comes in his Kingdom . . . and whatsoever the Saints, any of them do possess or enjoy of God in this life, *is only by faith.* (Lumpkin, 165, italics added).

Salvation is the gift of God, not of anything humans have manipulated. We cast ourselves on Christ, trusting that he, and not we ourselves, "is the author and finisher of our faith" (Heb. 12:2 KJV). Many Primitive Baptists take the issue of God's faithfulness so seriously that they are hesitant to suggest that they are "saved." Rather, they will often say that they "hope" that salvation has come to them. In this case hope does not mean wishful thinking but the "hope of salvation" in the work of Jesus Christ. If their hope for salvation is in Christ and not in themselves, that is their greatest security.

---

*Gerhard Ebelina, *Luther: An Introduction to His Thought* (Philadelphia: Fortress Press, 1970), 40.

Early Baptist practices also reflected the relationship between the individual and the believing community on the issue of conversion. Many Baptist congregations required that candidates for baptism testify publicly to their specific experience of grace, after which a group of church elders, clergy and laity, or the entire congregation, would vote on the validity of the conversion experience. That vote was a necessary prerequisite to the church's decision to offer baptism to new converts. While at first glance this may seem rather arbitrary, it was the congregation's way of saying that in the body of Christ, individual and communal relationships are essential. The Somerset Confession (1656) acknowledges the responsibility of the church in this statement:

> That in admitting of members into the church of Christ, it is the duty of the church, and ministers whom it concerns, in faithfulness to God, that they be careful they receive none but such as do make forth evident demonstration of the new birth, and the work of faith with power. (Lumpkin, 211)

The community was bound together by a covenant between God and the individual and the individual and the community of faith. This covenantal relationship united individuals with Christ and the community of the church. Churches would do well to find ways to recover that communal support for and response to the faith experienced by individuals. Perhaps the most biblical response to these issues is less "Am I saved?" than "Is my faith and trust in Christ?" the author of salvation.

33. What about good works?

The Bible is clear (?), "Faith without works is dead" (Jas. 2:17 KJV). "For by grace are ye saved, through faith, and that not of yourselves, it is the gift of God, not of works, lest any . . . should boast" (Eph. 2:8–9 KJV). Well, which is it, faith or works? Both, of course.

Roman Catholics have sought to clarify that question by clearly asserting that both faith and works are necessary for salvation. In reacting against what seemed certain extreme forms of Catholic "works righteousness" in the medieval church, Protestants placed renewed (dare we say re-formed) emphasis on *sola fide*, faith alone as the ground of true salvation. Martin Luther, the great Reformer, even suggested that the book of James was an "epistle of straw" because of its excessive concern for works and might best be stricken from the biblical canon.

At their best, Protestants have insisted that while the Christian pilgrimage begins with faith, good works are necessary to the fulfillment of Christ's continuing command to feed the hungry, cloth the naked, and care for the sick and imprisoned (Matt. 25). They are also one of the most important signs of genuine faith, a conversion from self-centeredness to an activist compassion and a gospel-induced commitment to alleviating human need. The Orthodox Creed of seventeenth-century General Baptists says it well:

> Yet the works of charity and mercy, must be minded as a duty to lend to the Lord, and pity and relieve the Lord's poor, weekly laying out for them, as god hath prospered us, according to our ability in freedom, liberality, and charity, according to our brethrens [sic] necessity, whether sick, or in prison, to visit and relieve them, and not only within the church, but to all as we do opportunity, and ability to do good. (Lumpkin, 324)

This statement is particularly important since it calls for benevolent action, not only to those within the covenanting community of the church but to those on the outside whose needs are also to be taken seriously and whose hurts should receive appropriate response.

In the nineteenth and twentieth centuries one of the great reassertions of the church's call to respond to the needs of the world around us came from Baptists such as Walter Rauschenbusch (1861–1918), who challenged Christians to take seriously the implications of the social gospel. While serving as pastor of a German Baptist immigrant congregation in the infamous Hell's Kitchen section of New York, Rauschenbusch called on the church to respond to the needs of the poor in an effort at *Christianizing the Social Order* (the title of his 1912 book), and to confront the implications of both personal and corporate sins born of the industrial revolution. His was a mandate for personal conversion to Christ and for bringing Christ's teaching to bear on social structures. For Rauschenbusch and other social gospelers, faith without works was not only "dead," it was theologically and personally impossible for followers of Jesus Christ.

7

Church

34. What is the nature of the church?

Baptists have a lot to say about the church. They begin by putting themselves within the stream of biblical descriptions for what the church is and/or ought to be. Thus such New Testament terms as *koinonia* (fellowship) and *ecclesia* (community) are essential to understanding the church's nature and calling. Baptists have often gravitated toward those great Pauline metaphors for the church, including people of God (bound to the long tradition of God's people), household of faith (a new family), and body of Christ (linked together inseparably). (That is not to say they have always agreed on what those terms mean in one local congregation!)

One of the most distinctive characteristics of the Baptist understanding of the church is that each congregation is a community of believers, those who can testify to an experience of God's grace in their hearts. The church on earth is composed not of all the baptized in a given locale or diocese but only of those who have claimed faith for themselves. This basic assertion distinguished Baptists from the prevailing approach of European Christianity that linked the church on earth to a religious establishment. To be born into a "Christian" state was to be baptized into a specific Christian communion. If the country or region was Catholic, Lutheran, Reformed, or Anglican, for example, then infants were baptized into the specific, dominant (established) church. Thus, citizenship and church membership were inseparable.

Baptists broke with all of that, constituting congregations where membership was granted not on the basis of citizenship or as a requirement by some state-based religious establishment but on uncoerced faith, experienced in the life of each person who claimed to be a disciple. This understanding of the nature of the church was there from the beginning. The English Declaration from Amsterdam (1611), written by the earliest band of General Baptists, says it plainly:

> The church of CHRIST is a company of faithful people I Cor. 1:2, Eph. 1:1, separated from the world by the word & Spirit of GOD, 2 Cor. 6:17, being knit unto the LORD, & one unto another, by Baptism, I Cor. 12:13, Upon their own confession of the faith, Acts 8:37, and sins, Matt. 3:6. (Lumpkin, 119)

A "confession" was the foundation for entry into the church and the basis for baptism.

The idea of a believers' church also meant that for some Baptists (not all) there was no distinction between the visible church on earth and the invisible church in heaven. What you saw on earth was what you got in heaven! That is why these Baptists were intent on evaluating, even approving, individual conversion experiences from within the entire community. The Particular Baptists' First London Confession says,

> Christ hath here on earth a spiritual Kingdom, which is the Church, which he hath purchased and redeemed to himself, as a peculiar inheritance: which Church, as it is visible to us, is a company of visible Saints, called & and separated from the world, by the word and Spirit of God, to the visible profession of the faith of the Gospel, being baptized into that faith, and joined to the Lord, and each other, by mutual agreement, [covenant] in the practical enjoyment of the Ordinances, [baptism and the Supper] commanded by Christ their head and King. (Lumpkin, 165)

The idea of a believers' church is the key to understanding the nature of covenant, congregational polity, conscience, and dissent. In short, it is the foundation of Baptist participation in what we know today as the free church tradition.

35. What is the nature of covenant?

Covenants bind us together. The way the Bible tells it, covenants were there in the beginning. God set a de facto covenant with Adam and Eve, detailing their duties—tend the garden, name the animals, eat of the "'fruit of the trees in the garden'" (Gen. 3:2), stay away from "'"the tree that is in the middle of the garden"'" (Gen. 3:3). The great covenant with Abraham established a relationship between God and a "peculiar people," the Hebrews. St. Paul indicates his belief that the church has been "grafted" into that covenant by virtue of Christ's sacrifice (Rom. 11:23).

The idea of covenant is an essential element for understanding the nature of the church in the free church/Baptist tradition. Baptists, most coming directly from seventeenth-century Puritanism, believed that the church's covenant was a two-way street. It began with God and salvation but was extended to the people of God, the church. It was both vertical—God's relationship with those who professed faith in Christ—and horizontal—the relationship shared by those believers who belonged to Christ and his church.

In colonial and frontier America many Baptist churches were founded on the basis of three guiding documents (along with Scripture): A confession of faith that said what they believed, a covenant that said how they would treat one another, and "rules of decorum" that said how they would conduct business. The New Hampshire Confession carries the idea of covenant into its article on the nature of the church, stating, "A visible Church of Christ is a congregation of baptized believers, associated by covenant in the faith and fellowship of the Gospel" (Lumpkin, 365).

In First Baptist Church, Highland Avenue, our home church in Winston-Salem, North Carolina, and the oldest African American Baptist church in town, we take Holy Communion every first Sunday of the month. Before the Communion service begins, we stand together, face another member of the congregation, and read aloud to each other the church's covenant, reaffirming our collective care and responsibility to the church, the world, and one another. It is a profound moment, when we feel our Baptist heritage dramatically!

36. What is the meaning of "church discipline"?

One of the more controversial aspects of the life of the church concerns the matter of church discipline, the effort to deal with members and/or issues that step outside the boundaries of Christian propriety, covenantal agreement, or doctrinal orthodoxy. Excommunication is perhaps the best-known ecclesiastical form of church discipline, particularly in the context of Roman Catholicism. As early as the year 325 at the Council of Nicaea, the creed declared of those who had an unacceptable view of the relationship of Jesus to God the Father, "These the Catholic and Apostolic Church anathematizes" (Bettensen, 36), meaning condemns and separates from.

The work of the congregation in verifying conversion experiences prior to baptism also had a disciplinary dimension. If the church could vote you in, it could also vote you out. Indeed, the possibility of disciplinary action is set forth in several of the seventeenth-century confessions of faith. Sometimes discipline meant restricting sinful Christians from the Lord's Table. As the Faith and Practice of Thirty Congregations (1651) details,

> If any one of the fellowship neglect the watching over his own heart, and so break out into an evil life and conversation, and all good means that God hath appointed hath been used towards such a one, and that person hath not performed, then ought not such a one to break bread with obedient walkers, to shew forth the death of Christ, seeing he doth deny him in life and conversation. (Lumpkin, 183)

The First London Confession of 1644 is even more specific about the possibility and necessity of discipline. It states that "Christ has likewise given power to his whole Church to receive in and cast out, by way of Excommunication, any member; and this power is given to every particular Congregation, and not one particular person, either member or office, but the whole" (Lumpkin, 168). In this confession it is the congregation alone that has the authority to discipline, indeed excommunicate, members.

Church discipline was strict and extensive in early Baptist churches, aided perhaps by the fact that congregations were small and discipline could have serious implications in families and communities of faith. As congregations expanded and numbers increased, monitoring disciplinary action became more complex. Also, one of the great problems of discipline, then and now, involves the difficulty of egalitarian justice given to all persons who get out of line. Baptists, like other Christians, soon found that discipline can turn into pettiness, particularly when carried out by the "group." As religious pluralism has become more normative and individuals can move from church to church and denomination to denomination rather easily, discipline becomes even more problematic. Persons disciplined in one congregation can simply join another, or, in the case of Baptists, start their own church. In the church, then and now, discipline is a worthy but terribly difficult matter.

37. What is the ecclesiology known as "Old Landmarkism"?

Old Landmarkism is a specific view of the nature of the church (ecclesiology) from a specific Baptist perspective that became particularly prominent in the nineteenth century and much of the twentieth, especially in the South and Southwest. It arose in Tennessee and Kentucky over the question of whether nonimmersed ministers could preach in Baptist churches. The conclusion of leaders such as Nashville's J. R. Graves (1820–1893) and Kentuckian J. M. Pendleton (1811–1891) was that such an action was inappropriate since non-Baptist members had a false baptism and a false view of the church and were therefore not part of the true church of Christ.

The name came from Prov. 22:28 (KJV): "Remove not the ancient landmark, which thy fathers have set." These distinguishing "marks of the true church" included congregational autonomy, believers' church, immersion baptism, closed communion (only members of local congregations could receive communion in those churches), and the belief that a succession of Baptist churches evident in historically dissenting groups had existed since New Testament times. Therefore the only true churches were Baptist churches, a line of churches that stretched in an unbroken line from Jesus' baptism in River Jordan by John *the Baptist.* As one old preacher is said to have declared, "Well, they didn't call him John the Presbyterian, now did they"?

Landmarkism bequeathed a decisive legacy to many Baptist communions, even those that did not receive its entire philosophy as normative for the church. It is one of the reasons that many Baptist churches continue to insist that those who have not received immersion must be "rebaptized" in order to be full members of a Baptist church, no matter how long they have professed faith in Christ. Landmarkism was one tool used by certain Baptists to prove that their church was the truest of the true. Unlike the other denominations that claimed a specific historic founder—Martin Luther, John Calvin, Ulrich Zwingli, or John Wesley—Baptists needed no such individual since they were formed in the initial Christian community by Jesus himself!

Landmarkism illustrates the continuing, though perhaps less volatile, debate over what constitutes the true church and how one identifies with it. It is one answer to the question of the basic marks of the church amid a growing Christian pluralism with multiple sects and denominations.

38. What is the role of the clergy in the church?

Baptists ordain ministers. Unlike the Quakers, their seventeenth-century counterparts, Baptists never rejected the ordination of individuals to the "gospel ministry." All of the confessions of faith from that period acknowledge the role of clergy in Baptist churches. The English Declaration at Amsterdam says,

The Officers of every Church or congregation are either Elders [pastors], who by their office do especially feed the flock concerning their souls, Acts 20:28 . . . or Deacons, Men and Women who by their office relieve the necessities of the poor and impotent brethren concerning their bodies, Acts 6:1–4. (Lumpkin, 121–22)

While some of the early Calvinistic Baptists followed the Reformed model of a four-fold church leadership—pastor, teacher, deacon, elder—most churches down to the present day have used two church officers: pastors and deacons. Pastors are the ordained clergy while deacons are a lay office chosen by the congregation to serve the spiritual, familial, and physical needs of persons. Some Baptist churches ordain deacons formally while others simply recognize them as elected for service without ordination.

Some seventeenth-century confessions, such as the Faith and Practise of Thirty Congregations, give attention to financial support of ministers, observing

that the maintenance of the Ministers which labour in the Word of God, ought to be the free and Charitable Benevolence, or the cheerful contribution of those that acknowledge themselves members of the same fellowship, [but warning that these] servants of God . . . ought to be content with necessary food and raiment, and to labour with their hands, that they may not be overchargeable, because they are to teach that doctrine to every member. (Lumpkin, 183–84)

Today most Baptist ministers receive some payment—full or part time—from the congregation in which they serve. Certain Baptist subgroups, such as the Primitive or Old Regular Baptists, reject the idea of a "hireling" ministry and require ministers to support themselves bivocationally.

John Smyth's Short Confession of 1610 contains a fine statement on the nature of ministry, applied to Baptists but appropriate for many Christian traditions. It reads,

In this holy church hath God ordained the ministers of the Gospel, the doctrines of the holy Word, the use of the holy sacraments, the oversight of the poor, and the ministers of the same offices; furthermore, the exercise of brotherly admonition and correction, and finally, the separating of the impenitent; which holy ordinances, contained in the Word of God, are to be administered to the contents thereof. (Lumpkin, 108)

Then and now the calling to become a vehicle of Word and sacrament is daunting, challenging, and difficult to a fault. The church should give careful attention to discerning those who are "fitly gifted and qualified by Christ . . . for the performance of the several duties, whereunto they are called" (Lumpkin, 212).

39. What is the priesthood of all believers?

At heart, Baptists are a peoples' church, committed to the Reformation idea of the priesthood of all believers and the idea that laypersons are called as agents of Christ on mission in the world. The priesthood of all believers affects Baptists in several ways. First, they agree with Martin Luther that "we have no priest save Christ himself" and each individual may come directly to God through Christ without any other earthly mediator. Each individual is responsible to God for faith or unfaith. Second, for Baptists, the priesthood of all believers is the doorway to freedom of conscience and the ability of baptized believers to read and interpret Scripture for themselves. Third, the priesthood of all believers does not mean that persons are free to believe anything they wish and still claim the name Baptist. Baptist communities of faith have the freedom, under the authority of Christ, to set boundaries that define Baptist identity and withdraw from those whose beliefs are not within those boundaries.

Although they ordain persons for "peculiar ministry" of Word and sacrament/ordinance, Baptists give serious attention to the idea that all persons could go directly to God without the need of any other human mediator. As a sign of this calling, certain early Baptists (some known as "Six Principle Baptists" because of the six identifying aspects of their belief and practice) offered the laying on of hands on two occasions in the church. The first was given to all the newly baptized as a sign of their calling to serve Christ, and the second as a way of "setting aside" pastors for specific churchly ministry. The Orthodox Creed describes that practice in this way: "Prayer, with imposition of hands by the bishop, or elder, [pastor] on baptized believers, as such, of the reception of the holy promised spirit of Christ, we believe is a principle of Christ's doctrine, and ought to be practiced and submitted to by *every baptized believer* in order to receive the promised spirit of the father and the son" (Lumpkin, 321, italics added). This two-fold laying on of hands was an outward symbol of the calling of each Christian believer to accept a call to ministry in the world.

In some Baptist communions, any person approved by the church may administer baptism and the Lord's Supper whether ordained or not. In other Baptist contexts, only duly ordained ministers or deacons can lead in those events.

4O. What about creeds?

"Baptists are confessional but not creedal." "We have no creed but the Bible." Those two statements, sometimes parallel, sometimes contradictory, have been used variously by Baptist groups in their effort to delineate specific doctrines but avoid hierarchical (top-down) imposition of beliefs. That is not to suggest that Baptists have been hesitant to delineate their doctrinal identity, at times by disciplining persons who were thought to have stepped outside the norm. Perhaps a more historically precise way of viewing Baptist practice would be to suggest that "Baptists are not creedal except when they decide to be."

Many Baptist groups past and present have often been hesitant to make formal use of the historic creeds of Christendom. While they might agree with the doctrines set forth in such documents as the Apostles', Nicene, or Athanasian creeds, they were hesitant to use these "man-made" documents lest they undermined or became a substitute for biblical authority and content. (The only seventeenth-century Baptist confession to mention and encourage use of the three creeds is the Orthodox Creed of General Baptists [1678].) This was due in part to the Baptists' commitment to "Scripture alone" as the guide for faith and practice, and in part because of their reaction to "coerced faith" of state-privileged religious establishments.

Nonetheless, from the earliest days of the Baptist movement churches have written confessions of faith, basic statements of belief and practice generally agreed on by groups of churches with particular theological distinctiveness. For the most part, these confessions reflected the division between Calvinist and Arminian approaches to theology. In other words, they each had a characteristically Baptist profile but differed on the theological interpretation of common beliefs and practices, so much so that they often contradicted one another.

Some Baptists reject the use of confessions altogether as detrimental to biblical authority as the only "rule of faith and practice" for Baptist churches. Others use confessions but with a disclaimer that they are not binding on the conscience of any believer who might differ with one segment or another. Still others gather their churches and denominations around such documents as an antidote to heresy and doctrinal laxity. Some compel congregational or denominational employees or board members to sign confessional documents as a part of their requirements for service. Differences arising from the historic fundamentalist-liberal controversies among Baptists have made questions of confessional "commitment" or "uniformity" a center of debate among many Baptist groups. Thus Baptists are not creedal, except when they decide to be or the times require them to be.

8

Worship and Sacraments/ Ordinances

41. What happens at Baptist worship services?

For Baptists, as for most other Christian traditions, worship is central to the life of the church. In these collective gatherings, Baptist people—in very diverse ways—celebrate the presence of God, sing praises, offer prayers, and gather around the Word of God for instruction, admonition, and biblical insight. Baptist worship, whatever its form, involves the centrality of preaching, the exegesis of and elaboration on biblical texts and their meaning past and present. Preaching is a vehicle for awakening sinners, instructing the community of faith, and waiting on the Word of God. Most, if not all, Baptists understand this as essential to Christian worship. The English Declaration at Amsterdam says that

> every Church ought . . . upon every first day of the week, being the LORDS day, to assemble together to pray Prophecie, [sic] praise GOD, and break Bread, and perform all other parts of Spiritual communion for the worship of God, their own mutual edification, and the preservation of true Religion, & piety in the church" (Lumpkin, 121).

Today, however, the format for putting those elements of common worship together varies considerably from church to church. Some Appalachian Baptist churches do not use musical instruments, sing in the "shaped note" style, require spontaneous preaching (no written sermons) from their pastors, and listen for the "holy whine" of the preacher's oral cadence. In services that reflect a greater formality of style ministers of other Baptist churches wear robes, follow the lectionary in their use of the biblical texts, and observe the Christian year, including Advent, Lent, Holy Week, and other annual liturgical events. Still others use a "praise and worship" approach, with music led by "praise teams" who sing "praise choruses," the words projected on screens throughout the congregation. Preachers, often in casual attire, may use Power Point technology, film clips, or other media resources to facilitate communication. Still other churches follow forms of worship characteristic of the revivalistic approach of an earlier Baptist era, with traditional hymns, prayer, "special music" by the choir, lengthy sermons (often with an evangelistic emphasis), and an "altar call" or "invitation to Christian discipleship" as a pivotal conclusion of the service. Many churches now offer multiple worship styles in services held at various times on a given Sunday.

These varied styles have not been without controversy in Baptist life. Churches continue to divide over what is sometimes called the "worship wars," divisions over which form of worship is most biblical or appropriate for a given congregation.

42. What about baptism?

Baptism by immersion is perhaps the most identifiable characteristic of the churches that call themselves Baptist. Early Baptists were Puritans, baptized as infants in the Anglican Church, who became convinced that infant baptism (the ecclesiastical norm in their day) was nowhere to be found in Holy Scripture and therefore was not a valid Christian ritual. They believed that baptism was to be given only to those who could profess to an experience of grace made known in Jesus Christ. In fact, they did not hesitate to reject all forms of the church that did not conform to that model. The English Declaration at Amsterdam (1611) unashamedly declared, "Every Church is to receive in all their members by Baptism upon the confession of their faith and sins wrought by the preaching of the Gospel, according to the primitive [biblical Instruction] . . . and practices. And therefore Churches constituted after any other manner, or of any other persons are *not according to CHRISTS Testament.* (Lumpkin, 120, italics added).

From their beginnings in 1609 until around 1641 these fledgling Baptist communities practiced baptism by affusion (drenching), pouring water three times on the head of the believer in the name of the Father, the Son, and the Holy Spirit. It was not until the 1640s that immersion—dipping the entire body in water—became the norm, a practice shared by all Baptist churches to this day. Immersion was normative enough by 1644 that it became an explicit part of the First London Confession of Particular Baptists. The statement reads,

> The way and manner of the dispensing of this Ordinance the Scripture holds out to be dipping or plunging the whole body under water; it being a sign, must answer the thing signified, which are these: first, the washing the whole soul in the blood of Christ: Secondly, that interest the Saints have in the death, burial, and resurrection; thirdly, together with a confirmation of our faith, that as certainly as the body is buried under water, and riseth again, so certainly shall the bodies of the Saints be raised by the power of Christ, in the day of resurrection. (Lumpkin, 165)

Baptists continue to speak of baptism in much the same way as their seventeenth-century forbears, an event that follows a profession of faith; involves immersion; and symbolizes the individual's new life in Christ; incorporation into Christ's body, the church; and identification with Christ in his death, burial, and resurrection. In one of the common statements made as the candidate is taken under the water ministers often say, "Buried with Christ in baptism, raised to walk in newness of life."

43. Does baptism "save" you?

While Baptists agree on the need for immersion baptism as the symbol of entry into Christ and his church, they do not always agree on its theological significance. Debates internal and external have sometimes surrounded the issue of whether baptism was "necessary" for salvation or whether baptism in any way conveys or participates in the process and accomplishment of salvation.

As far as I can discern, the seventeenth-century Baptist confessions of faith do not specifically address this issue. These early Baptists seem more concerned about issues related to the development of a believers' church and the requisite believers' immersion than with determining the relationship between baptism and salvation. In short, it is not that they believe baptism saves individuals but that they view salvation and baptism as inseparable. For them, baptism is a public profession of faith, inseparably linked to one's faith claims. They know it is a "sign" or a "symbol" that carries great power in demonstrating faith. The Orthodox Creed declares that "those which do really profess repentance towards God, and faith in, and obedience to our Lord Jesus Christ, are the *only proper subjects* of this ordinance" (Lumpkin, 317, italics added).

The question about baptism and salvation really took shape in the nineteenth century with the development of the restorationist movement, that effort to restore the New Testament church amid the growing debates over denominationalism. Restorationists, many related to the Stone-Campbell movement, suggested that they had reconstituted the true church as it was in the beginning and had been lost in sectarian divisions. They rejected denominational labels and wanted to call themselves "Christians Only," or simply "Disciples of Christ." Many Baptists "came over" to the restorationist churches. The followers of Alexander Campbell (1788–1866) were particularly strenuous in their assertion that baptism had regenerative implications for those who accepted Jesus as the Messiah. Baptists, many claiming that they were the only true New Testament church, insisted that baptism was "only a symbol" and had no salvific effect.

 ## 44. Can baptism be repeated?

From a theological point of view, multiple immersion baptisms administered in a believers' church are highly problematic. Baptism is a sacred event, made especially holy because it is administered in the name of God—Father, Son, and Holy Spirit. To repeat that name, potentially multiple times, over the same person is surely to "take the name of the Lord in vain." It is a practice that should be the absolute exception, not the norm, in Baptist churches.

Some persons request rebaptism after concluding that they were too young when they initially received immersion and did not understand what they were doing. Others have requested another immersion after concluding that they had not experienced genuine conversion. Some Baptist churches, influenced by the Landmark tradition, require immersion of all who come from nonimmersion traditions, even if those persons have been practicing Christians for many years. The practice of immersing longtime Christians remains controversial in Baptist life. Some churches insist it is the way to retain distinctive Baptist identity while other congregations have extended membership to longtime Christians who profess their faith, regardless of the mode of their initial baptism. If Baptist congregations choose to repeat the immersion of previously baptized Baptist church members, they should do so only after serious theological reflection. If repeat baptisms become normative in a Baptist community, the church may wish to revisit its evangelical theology and methods for introducing persons (especially children) to faith.

45. What is the meaning of the Lord's Supper?

In addition to baptism by immersion, Baptist churches celebrate the Lord's Supper as one of the essential sacraments/ordinances of the church, commanded by Christ. If baptism marks entry into faith, the Lord's Supper (Holy Communion) marks the Christian journey, the continuing symbol of Christ's presence with his people. Communion is celebrated in most Baptist churches either monthly, on the first Sunday, or quarterly, four times a year. Some Baptists, especially Primitive or Old Regular Baptists, prefer an annual Communion service only.

Certain seventeenth-century Baptist confessions of faith, namely the First London and the Somerset Confessions, do not even mention the Lord's Supper as an appropriate observance in Baptist churches! Other documents seem to divide over the meaning of the Supper, especially as concerns the presence of Christ in the bread and the wine. For example, both the Second London Confession (1688) and the Orthodox Creed (1679) deny the Roman Catholic idea of transubstantiation—that the bread and the wine actually become the very body and blood of the Lord Jesus. They also deny the Lutheran theology of "Real Presence," that Christ is both physically and spiritually present with the bread and wine.

Where Baptists themselves seem to divide is over the interpretation of Christ's presence in the Supper as viewed by the two Swiss reformers Ulrich Zwingli (d. 1529) and John Calvin (d. 1564). Calvinistic Baptists tend to stress Calvin's view of the Supper as conveying Christ's "spiritual presence," as noted in the Second London Confession:

> Worthy receiver, outwardly partaking of the visible Elements of this Ordinance, do then also inwardly by faith, really and indeed, yet not carnally, and corporally, but spiritually receive and feed upon Christ crucified & all the benefits of his death: the Body and Blood of Christ, being then not corporally, or carnally, but spiritually present to the faith of Believers, in that Ordinance, as the Elements themselves are to their outward senses. (Lumpkin, 293)

The Orthodox Creed on the other hand, notes,

> The supper of the Lord Jesus, was instituted by him . . . for the perpetual remembrance, and showing forth the sacrifice of himself in his death; and for the confirmation of the faithful believers in all benefits of his death and resurrection, and spiritual nourishment and growth in him. . . . The outward elements of bread and wine, after they are set apart by the hand of the minister, from common use, and blessed, or consecrated, by the word of God and prayer, the bread being broken, and wine poured forth, signify to the faithful, the body and blood of Christ, or holdeth forth Christ, and him crucified. (Lumpkin, 321)

Most Baptist churches in the United States made the change from fermented wine to unfermented grape juice in Holy Communion as a result of the impact of the temperance/total abstinence movement of the nineteenth and twentieth centuries. Some, particularly "mountain churches" in the Appalachian region, retained wine as the more literal and therefore the more biblical element in the celebration of the Lord's Supper. Some Baptist churches give significant emphasis to the Lord's Supper, while others tend to rush through it or insist that while its observance is a command of Christ for the church, it is simply a symbol or "reminder" of the work of Christ on the cross for the sins of the world.

46. Should Holy Communion be "open" or "closed"?

One of the oldest questions in Baptist life is whether Holy Communion should be open—given to all who profess faith in Christ—or closed—given only to those who have received baptism by immersion as a prerequisite, New Testament norm. To complicate matters further, some Baptists believe that only members of the specific local congregation in which the Lord's Supper is celebrated can take Communion when it is observed.

The proper response to this question is simply "yes." Since their beginnings in the early seventeenth century Baptists have divided over open/closed Communion. Quite simply, some congregations maintain that only immersed Baptists are valid recipients of the Supper in Baptist churches. Indeed, some require that only members of the local congregation may receive the Supper when it is offered. Still others have a historic sense that the Table belongs not to the individual church but to Christ himself, and no person who professes faith in him is to be turned away.

The fact is that many Baptist congregations have modified their original closed Communion views in order to establish an open Communion process that is implicitly, if not explicitly, enacted. Nonetheless, many conservative/fundamentalist Baptist churches continue to make closed Communion normative as a way of retaining what they believe to be the integrity of the Lord's Supper, believers' baptism, and the nature of the church from a Baptist perspective.

47. Is footwashing a sacrament?

Most Baptists would deny that the practice of footwashing could be considered a sacrament or ordinance on the same order as baptism or the Lord's Supper. However, footwashing is an observance practiced in a variety of Baptist communions including Primitive, Old Regular, and Free Will Baptists. Many of these groups view footwashing (based on John 13) as at least sacramental, if not a bona fide sacrament. The washing of feet is thus seen as a sign of humility and receptivity when Christians, like Jesus, take on the "form of a servant" (Phil. 2:6–7) and wash one another's feet, often in preparation for Holy Communion. As one Old Regular (Appalachian) Baptist woman comments, "I wouldn't take the bread and the wine if I didn't wash feet." Footwashing services create a powerful moment when Christian egalitarianism binds together people of high and low economic status in a symbol of servitude. For example, the Free Will Baptist Confession, a nineteenth-century document revised in 1948, lists footwashing as an "Ordinance of the Gospel" along with baptism and the Lord's Supper. The article states that footwashing is

> a sacred ordinance, which teaches humility, and reminds the believer of the necessity of a daily cleansing from all sin. It was instituted by the Lord Jesus Christ and called an 'example' on the night of His betrayal, and in connection with the institution of the Lord's Supper. It is the duty and happy prerogative of every believer to observe this sacred ordinance. (Lumpkin, 376)

48. What about "enthusiastical" worship?

Baptists are, in certain contexts, an "enthusiastical" people. Since the days of the Great Awakenings Baptists have made their spirituality public, with exuberant worship services where congregation and preacher respond to each other with shouts and other public signs of spiritual enthusiasm. Baptists have expressed their religion openly from the days of camp meetings and revivals in the eighteenth and nineteenth centuries. In those and similar settings believers shout, sing, and celebrate the presence of God in their hearts and amid the believing community. African American Baptist churches have often been characterized by the "answering congregation," a "call and response" between the preacher and the congregation. In such contexts, worship is not passive but engaging, with pastor and people engaging each other with the Spirit's enthusiasm. More recently, the influence of the charismatic movement has found its way into Baptist churches, with praise and worship as a context for enthusiastic singing and shouting, hands raised in praise to God and spiritual gifts cultivated in public worship and private prayer.

9

Bible

49. What's so special about the Bible?

"Jesus loves me, this I know, for the Bible tells me so." All religions have sacred books. All religions look to ancient texts to provide identity, continuity, and revelation. What makes the Bible special? My list of responses is purely my own—an effort to reflect on the Bible's place among us. First, the Bible—Hebrew and Christian texts—is claimed by three of the great religions of the world. Judaism set things in motion with the stories and details of God's covenant with a people; Christianity added a testament surrounding the revelation that the Messiah had come in the person of Jesus of Nazareth, who became to the church the Christ of God; Islam added a third testament incorporating elements of the first two and offering what Muslims believe to be the fullest revelation. All represent a wide biblical "family."

Second, through it all are the texts, for our purposes found in two of the three great monotheistic traditions: Judaism and Christianity. Those texts are special because they are believed to be the written revelation of the God of Abraham, Isaac, Jacob, and Jesus to the people of God.

Third, the Biblical texts have nurtured the faith of generations of faithful persons across the last three thousand years. They transformed lives, created communities, and sparked disputes that continue to the present day, energizing and dividing the people of God along the way.

Fourth, individuals and communities return again and again to the Bible because the biblical texts themselves are so amazing. They are at once simple and complex, reconciling and irreconcilable, consistent and contradictory, used and misused across the centuries. The biblical stories are lofty and earthy; they are great theology, spirituality, literature, and theater all at the same time. This dynamic is there from the beginning. God creates the first two people and puts them in charge of a garden. When they choose to disobey, lose innocence, and discover nakedness, God makes a set of clothes for them. And the stories only get better as the texts continue. At best, we allow the Bible to show us what we are and who God is, draw us back toward grace, write our own stories into those of the biblical texts, and, we Christians believe, live out the texts in our actions public and private, in light of the "Jesus Way." This inspiration is, as the Second London Confession notes, "the inward illumination of the Spirit of God . . . necessary for the saving understanding of such things as are revealed in the Word" (Lumpkin, 250). That is when the texts of the Bible become the Word of God to us.

50. How did we get the Bible?

The Bible is not one book. It is a collection of many texts that reflect the identity of two great world religions: Judaism and Christianity. The church's "first testament" was the Hebrew Bible, a collection of thirty-nine books from Genesis to Malachi. These contain the Pentateuch, the first five books of the Law, but continue with stories of the rise and fall of Israel, the poetry of the Psalms, the admonitions of Proverbs, and the declarations of the Hebrew prophets. Early Christians readily accepted the Hebrew Bible as an inspired guide for their new communities of faith. Early Christian writers cite many Old Testament passages to verify their work.

As the church took shape, a variety of "inspired" and informative writings appeared, some of which made their way into the New Testament "canon" or list of authoritative books and some of which did not. The twenty-seven books that constitute the New

Testament were written over a period roughly from 45 AD/CE (Thessalonians) to sometime in the early second century (John's Gospel). They contained the four Gospels and Acts, books that offer various accounts of the life, death, and resurrection of Jesus and the early days of the Christian church. Other books include various epistles detailing belief and practice in the first-century Christian communities. The book of Revelation is a visionary document that puts first-century issues and events in cosmic context.

As the canon took shape, the authority of the many writings was evaluated from multiple perspectives:

1. Was it "apostolic," that is, written by one of the apostles or in the tradition they represented?
2. Did the teaching, doctrine, or stories provided in the text offer the best and most authoritative instruction for the church?
3. Were the teachings included in these books verified in the churches even as they offered those churches the authoritative "rule of faith" for understanding and preserving the gospel of Jesus Christ?

Some have suggested that Baptists, like other Christians, have their own canon, a set of books and texts that are the focus of major emphases and interests that energized individuals and communities in the work of the gospel. While affirming the authority of the whole Bible, we all return again and again to texts that capture for us the essence of Christ's word and work. What is your canon within the canon?

51. What is the nature of biblical authority?

The English Declaration at Amsterdam (1611) says that

the scriptures of the Old and New Testament are written for our instruction, 2 Tim. 3:16 & that we ought to search them for they testify of CHRIST, John 5:39. And therefore to be used withal reverence, as containing the Holy Word of GOD, which only is our direction in al things whatsoever. (Lumpkin, 122)

The Standard Confession of General Baptists (1660) says that the Holy Scriptures represent "the rule whereby Saints both in matters of Faith, and conversation are to be regulated" (Lumpkin, 233). Generally speaking, contemporary Baptists would affirm both those statements.

Some of the early Baptist confessions have no specific statement on biblical authority—the First London Confession and the Standard Confession, for example, simply take it for granted. The Second London Confession has perhaps the lengthiest statement on the nature of biblical authority. Indeed, it begins with this opening comment: "The Holy Scripture is the only sufficient, certain, and infallible rule of all saving Knowledge, Faith and Obedience" (Lumpkin, 248).

For Baptists as for many other Christians the Bible is authoritative because

1. It is the vehicle of God's revelation to humankind.
2. It "testifies of Christ."
3. It is the "infallible rule" for doctrine, faith, and practice.
4. It "contains" (many Baptists would say "is") the "Holy Word of God."
5. It is the central authority for Baptist preaching and witness in the world.

Frontier Baptists in America often said it plainly: "The Bible says it, I believe it, and that settles it." Yet sorting out what the Bible says, what it means, and how it is to be applied is not easy. The full nature of biblical authority and interpretation is not always a source of unanimity among Baptists, sparking innumerable debates regarding certain modern categories for studying and interpreting the text and theories about the text. But amid these debates, Baptists unashamedly assert the authority of the Bible for the life of faith and the ministry and mission of the church.

Nonetheless, the Second London Confession did not hesitate to acknowledge the difficulties of discerning the full meaning of Scripture in all things, noting,

All things in Scripture are not alike plain in themselves, nor alike clear unto all; yet those things which are necessary to be known, believed and observed for Salvation, are so clearly propounded, and open in some place of Scripture or other, that not only the learned, but the unlearned, in a due use of ordinary means, may attain to a sufficient understanding of them. (Lumpkin, 251)

52. What is the meaning of biblical inerrancy?

The doctrine of biblical inerrancy is the belief that the Bible is without error in every topic it discusses. This errorless "truthfulness" includes not only issues of faith, doctrine, and morals but also natural and human history, science, and other subjects discussed in Scripture. Generally, those who hold to an inerrantist approach insist that given the discrepancies in the transporting and translating of the text across the centuries, the only truly inerrant documents were the "original manuscripts."

Support for the truthfulness of Scripture was essentially taken for granted by clergy and laity, Catholic and Protestant, throughout much of Christian history until certain scholars of biblical studies began to bring modern methods of literary, philosophical, and historical analysis to bear on biblical texts. This has led to a century-long conflict over the nature of Scripture and appropriate methods of interpretation. Inerrancy itself is not a uniform position. Some may hold to an implicit "dictation theory" whereby each word of Scripture came directly from God to the biblical writer (a view much like the Muslim understanding of the Koran's origins); some insist that it is inerrant in all areas; others see it as inerrant on matters of faith and doctrine only. Other Baptists reject inerrancy as a category of biblical interpretation but affirm the authority of Scripture as the "Word of God for the people of God."

For many Baptists, belief in the inerrancy of the Bible is a nonnegotiable that informs all other doctrines and interpretations.

Some go so far as to insist that one cannot be a Baptist without affirming that particular view of the biblical texts. Without it, they believe, all other doctrines grounded in Scripture are untrustworthy. Other Baptists refuse to affirm such a strenuous view of the nature of Scripture, not because they deny biblical authority but because they hesitate to bind the texts to one theory of interpretation. They suggest that because the Bible's inerrancy is based on the condition of the original manuscript and we do not possess such documents, the theory is a moot point. They insist that we deal with the texts we have rather than those we wish we had. Either way, the debate promises to continue, affecting relationships, doctrine, and ideas in Baptist communities of faith.

53. What do we mean by biblical hermeneutics?

Divisions over the nature, meaning, and application of theories of biblical inerrancy continue to divide Baptists and other Christians. In many respects, debates over biblical inerrancy compel Christians to confront the issue of hermeneutics, the method of interpretation they use to read and understand a text. Whether one has a particular theory of biblical inspiration or not, everyone has a hermeneutic, that is, the set or sets of glasses one uses to read and interpret a text. Sometimes those glasses are informed by the particular denominational or theological tradition—Roman Catholic, Eastern Orthodox, Protestant, Augustinian, Calvinist, Arminian, mystical, liberationist, or pentecostal—that claims one's loyalty. At other times location, politics, war, gender, or other cultural issues may influence biblical interpretation.

One of the most basic sets of hermeneutical methods used by Baptists and other Christian communions involves a response to the "argument from silence." In this method, one group says it this way: "Where the Bible is silent, we are silent." This means that the church will abide by no practice, however helpful or utilitarian, that is not explicitly discussed in the Bible. Primitive Baptists often reflect this principle, refusing to call their ministers "reverend," a term not used in Scripture, preferring the biblical title of elder. They refuse to use instrumental music in church because there is no sign of such actions in the New Testament churches. They reject elaborate denominational alliances or support for theological schools, mission boards, or even Sunday schools because they have no precedent in the "primitive" (earliest and most pristine) biblical communities.

An alternative hermeneutic is practiced by other Baptists who permit what the Scripture does not explicitly condemn. Thus ministerial titles, theological schools, denominational boards, robed choirs, organs, pianos, drums, and guitars are perfectly acceptable when they aid the church in fulfilling its mission in the world. These two principles clash considerably, especially on the grass roots level, as Baptist churches decide how to balance biblical literalism with the practical life of Christian action.

These hermeneutical influences provide ways of reading (and negotiating with) the biblical texts. Take the use of wine in communion, for example. Some Baptists insist on using fermented wine because that is the literal way of maintaining a biblically mandated practice. Others reject wine because it challenges another biblical teaching regarding the body as the temple of the Holy Spirit, a spiritual reality that wine might corrupt. Learning to listen to the hermeneutical language of specific groups can help us understand something about the way we read the Bible and seek to interpret it in the church and in our own lives. Likewise, the historical context of a particular understanding of biblical authority (or inerrancy) can condition a reading of the text that later generations reject or condemn. There is no more powerful illustration of that possibility than the way in which many Southerners used biblical texts, specifically passages such as Eph. 6:5–6, in defending slavery because it occurs in the Bible.

One of the real dangers of engaging in elaborate debates over specific theories of biblical inspiration (as important as these issues may be) is that if we are not careful the debates and the theories will distract us from the text. Biblical texts can be powerful, discomforting, and disarming, often taking readers where we do not wish to go. Distracting ourselves by intricate debates over theory may indeed represent our implicit and perhaps unrecognized attempts to hold a text at bay lest it overwhelm us with purposes we might well resist.

Another challenge for Protestants, especially Baptists, in the twenty-first century is to find a way to continue cultivating the study of the Bible. In an earlier day Baptist young people and adults were some of the most biblically literate individuals in America, due in large part to the strong presence of Sunday school, whose primary function was to teach the Bible in systematic, age-graded curricula almost from cradle to grave. Likewise, consistent participation in Sunday school created generations of persons who knew what the Bible said, even if they were less clear on what it meant. The loss of a Sunday-school generation in the early twenty-first century is one of the great challenges to Baptist (and other Protestant) attempts to continue to nurture future generations in knowing and loving the Bible.

54. What in the world is the "lectionary"?

In an age of declining biblical literacy, many Baptist ministers and churches are choosing to use the lectionary—that three-year cycle of guided reading through parallel texts from the Old Testament, the Psalms, the Gospel, and the Epistles—used by a variety of Christian communions. This cycle of Bible study and focus, developed in conjunction with the Christian Year—Advent, Epiphany, Lent, Holy Week, Easter, and Pentecost—offers the opportunity for preacher and congregation to revisit texts, often confronting texts that might otherwise be ignored or avoided.

Some Baptists will never, ever use the lectionary since for them it smacks of "high church" or mandated ways of preaching that thwart the free movement and inspiration of the Spirit. It simply would not work. Truth is, however, every church develops its own lectionary of sorts, revisiting texts again and again across the years.

As the difficulties surrounding biblical content increase, as they surely will, Baptist churches may need to consider the use of the lectionary as one way (among many) for teaching the faithful the nature and content of the biblical story. It could become a valuable tool for carrying a congregation through the Holy Scriptures in an orderly, intentional way. (Perhaps the "elders" should give it some thought.)

1🔾

Theology

55. How do Baptists "do theology"?

Given Baptist theological diversity, a better way to ask this question might be, How do Baptists "do *theologies*"? In other words, different Baptists approach core theological beliefs from a variety of biblical and doctrinal perspectives. As we have already noted, Baptists essentially began at both ends of the Protestant theological spectrum, Arminian and Calvinist. Some developed around Arminian ideas supporting general atonement, free will, falling from grace, and the cooperation of grace and human choice in bringing about salvation. Others remain thoroughgoing Calvinists, promoting limited atonement, total depravity, unconditional election, and perseverance of the saints. Still other Baptist groups have been influenced by the holiness, charismatic, inerrantist, evangelical, fundamentalist, liberal and social gospel movements.

Baptist theologians have written theology that reflects varying opinions of classic Christian doctrines and disputes. At the same time, much of Baptist church life is shaped by a popular or "peoples" theology that is influenced by worship styles, regionalism, race, politics, and cultural norms that shape basic practices if not traditional beliefs.

Early Baptists did not hesitate to make their theological positions known, challenging those inside and outside the Baptist fold whose views they felt to be theologically and doctrinally inadequate. Clearly, theology is one important reason there are so many different Baptist groups in the United States. Some Baptist-related theological perspectives are highly speculative, austere, and pietistic, often reflecting a degree of mystical encounter with God. Other Baptists claim little interest in formal theology, insisting that their views merely exemplify the same doctrines and practices of the New Testament church, the only source of biblical orthodoxy.

While Baptists have written formal statements of theology since their beginnings in the seventeenth century, there is also a sense in which the local congregation, composed of both clergy and laity, remains a source of theological interpretation and conversation on the most basic level of Baptist life. Thus Baptists tend to test their theology by Scripture, Baptist doctrine, and the beliefs and practices of their specific congregations. In this way Baptists do not hesitate to express their theological opinions, air them freely, and divide when necessary.

A brief survey of the theological perspectives of varied Baptist groups includes the following:

1. All Baptists would readily insist that they do theology from a biblical perspective. The Bible is the central authority for all theological perspectives.
2. Primitive or Old Regular (Appalachian) Baptists do theology from a strict Calvinist perspective that stresses God's sovereignty in election and predestination.
3. Fundamentalist Baptists do theology from the standpoint of certain nonnegotiable dogmas, including biblical inerrancy and the virgin birth, sacrificial atonement, and bodily resurrection of Jesus Christ.
4. Landmark Baptists combine fundamentalist theology with a specific perspective on the nature of Baptists as representing the only true church.
5. African American Baptists often do theology as shaped by biblical and liberationist responses to their histories in slavery, segregation, racism, and the struggle for civil rights.
6. Liberal Baptists often shape theology as influenced by modern biblical and sociological studies, feminist studies, ecumenical relationships, and the social gospel.
7. Evangelical Baptists may combine various theological traditions in an effort to offer a more "moderate" conservative

response to divisive theological questions of Scripture, tradition, social action, and doctrine.

56. Are Baptists "conservative" or "liberal"?

One easy answer to that question would be simply "yes." Baptists are primarily conservative in theology and practice but with a significant liberal streak on a variety of social or humanitarian issues. On the other hand, Baptist theology, with a few exceptions, often seems to be spectrum stretching, from extreme conservatism to modified conservatism to occasional liberalism on theological matters. Baptist conservatism itself is not monolithic, and Baptists may surprise themselves when it comes to specific issues they affirm or challenge. For example, historically conservative Baptists have sometimes taken surprisingly liberal or even radical positions related to religious liberty, the social gospel, and, especially in the case of African American Baptists, the civil rights movement. Theological liberalism took shape from the late nineteenth century and remains a presence in certain segments of the Baptist family. Other more conservative Baptists quickly deny that liberalism can legitimately claim a place in Baptist identity. From the perspective of many liberal groups outside the Baptist fold, these divisions appear to be degrees of conservatism rather than thoroughgoing liberalism.

57. What is the role of education in Baptist life?

Historically Baptists have often seemed to have a "love/hate" relationship with education. On one hand, they have founded schools—colleges, universities, seminaries—for the training of their young people. On the other, they often communicated their concern that certain educational approaches—some existing in their own Baptist-related schools—would somehow "steal the faith" out of a new generation of Baptist youth. As one frontier Baptist was alleged to have remarked, "We don't believe in an educated ministry; we saw what it did to the Presbyterians!" Nonetheless, Baptist higher education began in America with the founding of the College of Rhode Island (later Brown University) in 1764. By the mid-nineteenth century Baptist-related colleges stretched from Maine to Texas.

These schools often confronted controversies over educational approaches and subject matter from biblical studies to science and from theatrical productions to admissions policies. In recent years, especially in the South, many colleges and universities founded by Baptists have either deepened or broken those connections with their parent bodies, often over controversies related to theology, governance, and campus life. While Baptist commitment to higher education remains strong, debates continue to rage over the nature of "Christian" higher education in a discernibly Baptist context.

58. Why is theology important?

Theology is important because all Christian communities need identity. There really is no "generic" theology, beliefs unattached to specific ideas, personal, communal, and historical. Knowingly or unknowingly, all religious communities have a theology. Some are simply more intentional about that theology than others. Whatever form it may take, theology is important for numerous reasons.

First, theology helps us understand who we are as Baptist Christians. It provides complete definitions or general outlines of what we believe and what those beliefs mean. Second, it gives us a place to stand within the world and the church. One might hope that theological identity would sustain a kind of "hospitable traditionalism" that offers believers a place to stand, not to turn inward on themselves but outward in response to the needs of the world in the name of Jesus Christ. Third, theology is important because beliefs link us with a community and a history. As we have noted throughout this book, there are multiple theological perspectives expressed in historic documents written from the very beginning of the Baptist movement. While these documents may not articulate the exact beliefs of every Baptist who affirms them (chances of that are nil, by the way), they remind us that Baptists do have historic identities that have been formed in the crucible of struggle, celebration, debate, and freedom of thought.

Fourth, in our pluralistic era, efforts at openness and dialogue should not be developed at the expense of serious theological differences. Beliefs matter and should not be trivialized in an effort to compel community. The real question may be whether we can communicate and confront common human need even as we recognize that some of our theological differences are irreconcilable. We aren't very good at striking that kind of balance. But we can keep trying.

59. How does Baptist theology differ from other theologies?

In a sense, Baptist theology is not terribly unique. Many churches and denominational groups now practice believers' baptism by immersion, govern themselves through the congregation, believe the Bible is the authoritative word of God, and promote the priesthood of the laity. In other ways, Baptists are unique in the way that they link those identifying characteristics. Clearly, Baptists have declared themselves about the nature of the church, the nature of faith, and the meaning of the gospel. They reject Episcopal and Presbyterian forms of church government, challenge religious establishments (even if they cannot agree on which establishments), and, in some cases, encourage believers to "speak their minds" on issues of theology, Scripture, and practice.

Baptists are difficult to categorize. Some Baptists continue to emphasize the uniqueness of their doctrines and draw clear lines of demarcation between themselves and other (some would say lesser) Christian groups. Others run to ecumenical dialogue and even interfaith communication in an effort to find common ground for prayer, worship, and service in the world. In essence, Baptists are not "hierarchical" and often represent a peoples' movement that gives attention to the people on the margins of society and church life. As noted earlier, they write theology from the "bottom up," meaning that they are, at best, concerned about the role of the individual in confronting common problems. For better or for worse, Baptists really are a theological peoples' movement.

60. How does theology influence ethics?

Theology ultimately involves praxis. It defines how persons live and move in the church and the world. Baptists have often been outspoken advocates of certain ethical positions, based on certain central doctrinal and theological tenets that could not be neglected. In the nineteenth century, abolitionist Baptists attacked slavery as the ultimate denial of Christ's most basic teaching, "Thou shalt love thy neighbor as thyself." Pro-slavery Baptists, however, defended the South's "peculiar institution" on the basis of certain biblical texts and the admonition to treat slaves with kindness as commanded in Scripture.

Early Baptists generally permitted church members to use alcoholic beverages in moderation, noting the use of wine in various biblical contexts. Later Baptists defined total abstinence from alcohol as a requirement of all who would be truly committed followers of Jesus Christ. Theological conviction leads many Baptists to oppose "worldliness" in many forms, including gambling, prostitution, dancing, smoking, alcohol use, pornography, abortion, homosexuality, long hair on men, short hair (and skirts) on women, Sunday shopping, war, exploitation of the environment, gun control, lack of gun control, and a variety of other personal and communal behaviors.

While a majority of Baptists tend toward conservative responses to public and private morality, they also divide over strategies or emphases in addressing many issues. Today, for example, many Baptists differ less on whether environmental problems such as pollution deserve immediate care and attention than on the theological basis for understanding the nature of the physical universe as taught in Holy Scripture. Contemporary Baptists increasingly differ not on whether unfaithfulness in marriage relationships might be permitted but on whether monogamous relationships evident among homosexual couples are comparable to those of heterosexual couples. Some Baptist groups and individuals, no doubt a majority, oppose any homosexual behavior as inappropriate to Christians, while others, a definite minority, consider themselves "open and affirming" to those who seek monogamous same-sex unions.

Such differences raise the question of church discipline in Baptist church life. In earlier periods, Baptists did not hesitate to bring public discipline to bear against members they felt had stepped outside the boundaries of Christian propriety. During the nineteenth and early twentieth centuries, Baptist churches frequently expelled members for a variety of public and private sins. Some churches used the terms of the church covenant to set theological and moral standards of discipline for members. Discipline was practiced not only in response to inappropriate behavior but as a theological response to violation of a communal and spiritual relationship between the church and the individual. Yet the difficulties of maintaining standards that were applied to all church members, the tendency of some disciplinary actions to turn to pettiness, and the possibility of major church schisms over such efforts led many congregations to forego public practices of discipline. Today, a growing concern about "worldliness" in the church has led some Baptist churches to revisit the issue of public discipline of church members in an effort to protect the reputation and witness of the church in an increasingly secular society.

11

Church and State

61. What is the nature of religious liberty?

One of the most distinctive characteristics of the people called Baptists is their commitment to religious liberty. In fact, seventeenth-century Baptists in England and America were among the first religious communions to call for radical religious freedom without sanction from church or state. Thomas Helwys, one of the early founders, wrote an important treatise known as *The Mystery of Iniquity* (1612). Helwys was one of the first Baptists to insist that God alone was judge of conscience, and therefore neither state nor church could judge the conscience of the heretic (who believed the wrong things) or the atheist (who believed nothing at all). He insisted that all persons, not simply Christians, had such freedom: "Let them be heretics, Turks, Jews, or whatsoever, it appertains not to the earthly power to punish them in the lease measure" (Helwys, 53).

This idea is the foundation of religious liberty and pluralism in Western society. The Standard Confession says it clearly:

> It is the will, and mind of God (in these Gospel times) that all men should have the free liberty of their own consciences in matters of Religion, or Worship, without the least oppression, or persecution, as simply upon that account; and . . . for any in Authority to otherwise to act, we confidently believe is expressly contrary to the mind of Christ." (Lumpkin 232–33)

62. What are the theological roots of religious liberty?

For Baptists, the roots of religious liberty lie in the concept of a believers' church. If the church is to be composed of persons who have professed faith in Christ for themselves, then uncoerced faith is essential to genuine religious experience. Therefore, no state- or church-sanctioned requirements that attempt to coerce faith through an implicit or explicit established religion (enforcing attendance, baptism, or other types of religious conformity) is acceptable under God. The Orthodox Creed builds its concept of conscience on the basis of Christ's saving work on the cross, noting that Christ "would not have the consciences of men in bondage to, or imposed upon, by any usurpation, tyranny, or command whatsoever, contrary to his revealed will in his word." It concludes that "the requiring of an implicit faith, and an absolute blind obedience, destroys liberty of conscience, and reason also, it being repugnant to both" (Lumpkin, 331–32).

The Standard Confession noted that Christians are to be "subject to the higher Powers," but warned that if the state should at "any time impose things about matters of Religion, which we through conscience to God cannot actually obey, then we with Peter also do say, that we ought . . . to obey God rather than men . . . yet humbly purposing (in the Lords strength) patiently to suffer whatsoever shall be inflicted upon us, for our conscionable forbearance" (Lumpkin, 233). Many early Baptists anticipated persecution for their views (and often received it)!

Thus historic Baptist response to religious liberty began with the commitment to a believers' church grounded in the promise of uncoerced faith and freedom of conscience. All persons were responsible only to God for the faith they did or did not have. And because conscience was formative for religious decision making and state or official churches often tried to coerce conscience, then dissent in behalf of liberty was inevitable. Baptists did not necessarily expect their views to be made normative in the state, but they expected that the state would not persecute them or any others for giving voice to their views in the public square.

63. What do Baptists mean by a "religious establishment"?

A religious establishment is any religion that receives special privileges or status from the state, thereby occupying, implicitly or explicitly, a unique place over other religions in the society. In the European society in which Baptists were formed was a sea of religious establishments—Catholic, Anglican, Reformed, and Lutheran. In colonial America religious establishments existed in New England and the South until the early nineteenth century.

Today, many Baptists in the United States disagree over the nature of implicit, de facto religious establishments. Some suggest that secularism has become the unofficial established religion of twenty-first-century America, privileging "secular humanism" and attempting to restrict religious influences in schools, politics, and the public square. These Baptists believe that Christian voice and values are being undermined at every level of social and political life. Their dissent, therefore, is against the secularization of society and its impact on religion.

Other Baptists warn that America has long privileged religious majorities—Baptists in the South, Mormons in the West, or Catholics in the East—often in subtle but distinct ways. These Baptists insist that radical religious liberty as articulated by their Baptist forbears requires them to oppose attempts at securing privilege from the state for anyone's religion or religious views. Often known as "separationists" these Baptists insist that government intervention in church- or faith-based issues can lead to compromise by the church in ways destructive to the gospel it proclaims. Pluralism means that no one is silenced and everyone has the right to speak and promote his or her religious views, but not with the help of the state, implicitly or explicitly. They point to the long heritage of Baptists fighting for religious liberty and warn that such hard-fought freedom can be lost in the temptation to secure privileged status in state and society. These differences of opinion have raised considerable debate inside the Baptist house, divisions that show no signs of abating.

64. Is there such a thing as a "Christian nation"?

This question, as old as the Republic, finds Baptists on both sides. Some Baptists say yes; others, no, with many individuals on either side of the argument making their case forcefully. Some Baptists believe that God indeed chose America to be a beacon of liberty and godliness to the world, a "City on a hill, and a "Righteous empire." These Baptists generally support prayer in schools, posting the Ten Commandments in public buildings, and receiving faith-based funding in church-related social or educational programs. They suggest that while America has often failed to live out its calling as a divinely chosen nation, it is nonetheless the nation's destiny to live up to that calling under God. Many of these folks believe that the loss of the idea of "Christian nation" explains the deterioration of morality and Christian virtues in the new American marketplace.

Other Baptists agree with the erstwhile Baptist founder Roger Williams, who denounced the idea four hundred years ago, asserting that there are no Christian nations, only Christian people, bound to Christ by faith, not citizenship. These Baptists generally oppose prayer in schools, tax-funded vouchers for use by parochial schools, or any formal governmental support—state, local, or national—that appears to privilege any one religion or sectarian group. They insist that claims of "Christian nationhood" open the door to moral and spiritual compromise when nations act in ways that contradict or negate the teachings of Christ related to the marginalized, war, slavery, and economic exploitation. Debates over this issue and its implications for national identity and ecclesiastical responsibility promise to continue for years to come.

65. Should pastors or churches take political positions?

Of course not, at least not in ways that put pressure on members to vote in particular ways. However, the line between conviction and political endorsement can often seem very thin in the heat of political campaigns. In many communities, political leaders sometimes make visits to church worship services, especially during election season. Some churches have been known to post the "Christian" voting record of candidates as a way of informing church members about the action of politicians on religiosocial issues. Some pastors urge members to support certain moral crusades—anti-abortion, civil rights, environmentalism, or opposition to gambling—that involve specific ways of casting a ballot. Some Baptist churches have long taken public stands related to sociopolitical issues from temperance to anti-abortion to civil rights.

Martin Luther King Jr. guided the Montgomery, Alabama, bus boycott from the pulpit of the Dexter Avenue Baptist Church. While the organization he founded for accomplishing that effort, the Southern Christian Leadership Conference, was a freestanding nonprofit organization, it did reference "Christian" in its title. During the early twentieth century, J. Frank Norris, nationally known fundamentalist Baptist from Texas, did not hesitate to attack politicians and other community leaders he felt to be corrupt, preaching sermons like one titled "The Ten Biggest Devils in Fort Worth, Names Given." Discerning the role of the church in political issues and participation in the public square is no easy matter. Baptists will doubtless struggle with these issues even as they seek to live faithfully with their consciences and their Christian commitments.

Throughout American history Baptist church members have gone to jail for reasons of conscience related to a variety of social and ethical issues. These days, the government regulations regarding tax-exempt status for churches serve to complicate matters considerably when congregations or their pastors exercise political opinions or respond collectively to divisive political issues within the context of the church.

12

Christian Life

66. What do Baptists believe about the saints?

Baptists, like many Protestants, believe that all Christian believers are "saints," made holy and distinct through "Jesus Christ their Head, by his Spirit, and Faith," as the Second London Confession declares. By their profession of faith, saints "are bound to maintain a holy fellowship and communion in the worship of God, and in performing such other spiritual services, as tend to their mutual benefit" (Lumpkin, 289–90). Early Baptists rejected Roman Catholic theology regarding the "merits of the saints" and the belief that certain Christians, now departed, constitute a peculiar segment of the church whose miraculous graces are beneficial beyond their deaths and who, admitted uniquely to God's presence, are able to intercede for others who seek their aid.

In response to that idea, Baptists asserted that the priesthood of all believers meant that individuals come directly to God through Christ without additional mediators in this world or the next. All those who come by faith thus become part of the "household of faith," the communion of saints (Lumpkin, 290).

67. What do Baptists believe about "Christian perfection"?

Any discussion of "Christian perfection" must begin with Baptist understanding of the nature of conversion. Whatever else they may believe, Baptists generally agree that the Christian journey begins with conversion, a conscious decision to "accept Jesus Christ as savior" and receive baptism into his body, the church. Conversion is the primary religious experience for many Baptists, the process of entering into faith. Sanctification, going on in grace, represents the calling of all who are truly "born again," a nonnegotiable life of Christian discipleship for all baptized believers. Particular or Calvinist Baptists link justification and sanctification as spiritual events that occur at conversion, as symbolized in the washing of baptism. Free Will and General Baptists, however, are more prone to use "perfectionist" terminology as the sign of continuing Christian discipleship that is necessary to keep one from "falling from grace."

While Baptists generally would not use the term "perfection" to describe their understanding of the nature of postconversion Christian living, they are indeed clear about their belief that Christians are to remain free from sin and reflect the great moral qualities of the gospel. They are less likely than some other groups to believe that sanctification is a "second work of grace." Instead, they believe it is present in conversion, empowering members to follow Christ in daily living. The Short Confession of 1610 says that while certain Baptists are scattered throughout the world, they belong to the body of Christ by justification by faith.

For many Baptists, justification and sanctification are closely linked. To be in Christ is to be sanctified. The task of the church is to teach and guide believers in Christian living and growth in grace. Perfection is less the issue than is following Christ across a lifetime. As the Short Confession (General Baptist, 1610) suggests, those "justified by faith, liveth and worketh by love (which the Holy Ghost sheddeth into the heart) in all good works, in the laws, precepts, ordinances given them by God through Christ." By doing that the Christian "praiseth and blesseth God, by a holy life" (Lumpkin, 108).

68. Why do we pray?

Baptist piety is deep, born of a direct experience with Jesus Christ in conversion and profession of faith. Baptists pray because of that relationship with Christ, because of the need to bring their praise and hurts to "the throne of grace," and because of a strong belief that God answers prayer. The Orthodox Creed says that "prayer is an holy, religious, and sacred ordinance of God, and the duty of all men to perform, by the law of God" (Lumpkin, 328). It also advises that all prayer and worship should occur "at least two times a day" in the lives of all genuine Christians.

Frontier Baptists instituted "prayer meetings," often conducted midweek by laity in the absence of the bivocational or part-time ministers. Prayer meetings continue to this day in many churches in services devoted to voicing the needs and concerns of the congregation and praying specifically about them together.

From frontier times, individuals who seemed particularly gifted as "prayer warriors" have been recognized in Baptist congregations. These men and women, often longtime Christians, are sometimes known as persons who "know how to get hold of God," persons whose purity of life and devotion to Christ make them exemplary witness to the power of prayer. For Baptists, as for many Christians, prayer is an important sign of intimacy with God, a way of deepening relationship with the Divine, and a means of intercession for personal, familial, communal, and global needs—physical, material, spiritual, and personal.

 ### 69. What about divine healing?

Baptists believe strongly in divine healing. They pray to that end for those they know and do not know. As a whole, Baptists have not generally developed the kind of "faith healing" theology and practice evident in many pentecostal churches. Nonetheless, the possibility of divine healing is a major element in Baptist piety, a major goal of intercessory prayer. Baptist churches across the theological and regional spectrum engage in prayer for the healing of persons in their congregation and around the world. The work of God in healing through miracle, medical procedures, and personal self-care is a major part of the spiritual life of Baptist communities of faith.

At the same time, Baptists have generally stayed away from the more public "healing lines" evident in certain pentecostal faith-healing practices. Many Baptist clergy and laity point to certain miraculous, unexplainable instances when healing occurs. They may also point out the way in which physicians, hospitals, and new medical discoveries participate with God and the faithful individual in bringing about healing. More recently, some Baptist congregations have used the practice of "anointing with oil" for the sick and the dying as a sign of God's healing presence, whatever the ultimate physical outcome may be.

Some Baptist ministers and professors have become increasingly concerned about the so-called "health and wealth gospel" in which certain preachers appear to promise healing (and material prosperity) as almost an entitlement for all those who have genuine faith. This emphasis is seen by many as an overstatement that may create spiritual and psychological confusion for desperately ill people. Debates over the "health and wealth gospel" will no doubt continue for some time, particularly because of the link that is sometimes created between promised healing and financial contribution to specific ministries.

70. What is the relationship of evangelism to the Christian life?

Not all Baptists are evangelistic in the sense of an obligation of every disciple to "share the gospel with the lost." Some Baptists—certain Primitive or Old Regular Baptists—believe that evangelist efforts to convert sinners on the spot are little more than "works righteousness," futile attempts on the part of human beings to usurp the saving power known only to God. Nonetheless, a large number of Baptists believe that personal witness to Jesus Christ, often in direct conversation with persons who have never had a "personal experience" with Christ, is essential to all who would claim to be Christians. True Christians, therefore, would want to retell "the old, old story, of Jesus and His love" to as many people as possible. In many regions of the country, Baptists are known for their "personal evangelism," through presenting the "plan of salvation" to as many persons as possible and calling on them to come to Christ immediately.

Some Baptists agree with the need to evangelize as part of their Christian witness but prefer to be less direct, often speaking of "lifestyle evangelism," in which acts of compassion and selfless Christian living in the marketplace draw non-Christian individuals to the faith without aggressive and sometimes "impersonal" personal evangelism. Whatever the explicit method, many Baptists believe that the truth of one's Christian faith and life of discipleship is evidenced by the imperative to present the gospel to the entire world, if necessary, one person at a time. For them, Christian discipleship is inseparable from Christian witness.

13

Reign of God

71. What does "eschatology" mean?

Eschatology is the study of "last things," the stories and ideas surrounding the end of the age, the culmination of the world as we know it. Eschatology is nothing new, although there are numerous new ways of introducing it for public consumption. (The recent, best-selling "Left Behind" series of books is a case in point.) Eschatology is no real surprise to persons in the Judeo-Christian tradition, for both testaments of the two religions give evidence of eschatological speculation by a variety of persons, many of whom expected the imminent end of their age. This is true of the book of Daniel in the Hebrew Bible and the book of Revelation in the Christian Scriptures. Jesus himself anticipated the coming "end of the age" when a new rule and reign of God (kingdom of God) would dawn on the world. Jesus was a harbinger of that new day.

For Christians, the "eschatological hope" involves the belief that

1. It really is God's world.
2. Evil and destruction may prevail for a time, but in the end God's will and work will prevail.
3. God is the ultimate source of human history, present at the beginning and the end.
4. In the end, God will set things right.

In its most basic sense, eschatology is grounded on hope—the assurance that it really is God's world, God will have the last word, and that word will be good. Justice and peace will become the order

of the day, and nations will "study war no more." With that great
hope, the church continually prays, "Even so, come, Lord Jesus."

72. What about the second coming of Jesus Christ?

For many Baptists (and other Christians) the return of Jesus Christ
is a dramatic event that punctuates or sets in motion the end times.
The Standard Confession of 1660 says that the "same Lord Jesus who
shewed himself after his passion . . . *shall so come in like manner as
he was seen go into Heaven*, Acts 1:9–11" (Lumpkin, 231).

Much speculation has surrounded the particulars of this return
based on various readings of a collection of biblical texts. Those
who view those texts literally would generally agree that

1. No one knows the "times or the seasons" (Acts 1:7; 1 Thess.
   5:1).
2. Christians should learn to read the "signs of the times" in
   anticipation of Christ's coming (Matt. 16:3).
3. The event will represent a dramatic moment in history (Phil.
   2:10).
4. It will set in motion an end to the old world and the beginning
   of a new one (Rev. 21:1).

Over the centuries, some persons have developed intricate theories regarding the nature of the end times as set forth in these and
other books. Some associate the "end time" with the millennium
mentioned in Rev. 20 when the dead who had testified for Jesus
"came to life and reigned with Christ for a thousand years" (Rev.
20:1–6). Millennial theories that have long been a part of the
church and the life of the Baptists include the following:

> *Postmillennialists* believe that Jesus will return *after* the mil-
> lennium, a thousand years of spiritual renewal and peace,
> much of it brought in by the church on earth. Some early
> Baptists saw the Great Awakenings as a sign of the post-
> millennial return of Christ. Many colonial revivalists like
> Jonathan Edwards were postmillennialists.

Premillennialists believe that the world will grow worse and worse until the triumphant Christ intervenes, defeats his spiritual enemies (Satan and his followers), and reigns for a thousand years before the culmination of history. Some premillennialists point to the "rapture" as a time before, during, or after "the Great Tribulation" when the saints living and dead are taken out of the world. Not all agree on exactly when that will take place in the "final days." Premillennialism is perhaps the most popular theory of the end time among contemporary Baptists.

Amillennialists suggest that the millennium is a symbolic number not to be read as a literal element of the last times. Rather, God will speak an end to history in God's own time and God's own way. Many Baptists in the early to mid-twentieth century held to amillennial views.

Across the years many Baptists have been caught up in millennial fervor in a variety of movements, some of which understood that Christ's return was imminent. When it did not occur according to their immediate predictions, they were forced to develop other ways of understanding the issues or expanding the predictions. Many Baptists participated in the "fifth monarchy movement" of the late 1600s in England, a group that saw the English Civil War as a prelude to Christ's immediate return. Some joined the Baptist preacher William Miller (1792–1849) in anticipating Christ's return between 1843 and 1844 and were again disappointed. The twentieth century saw similar predictions and debates, many of which continue into the twenty-first century. Evangelists from Dwight L. Moody to Billy Graham to Jerry Falwell predicted the imminent end of the age as they called for sinners to turn to salvation.

73. What and where is the kingdom of God?

The idea of God's rule and reign is essential to an understanding of the "kingdom of God" and its anticipation by the church of Jesus Christ. It suggests that God is ultimately in control and in the end all things will be brought under that rule, with God's will established "on earth as it is in heaven" (Matt. 6:10). The concept is evident in the Hebrew expectation of the coming "Day of the Lord," when all will be set right (Amos 5:18–20; Isa. 11:1–9).

The kingdom of God is a phrase that echoes throughout the Gospels. Jesus spoke of it with great frequency and is described as "preaching the gospel of the kingdom" (Matt. 4:23 KJV). Many of his parables are aimed at illustrating the nature of a "kingdom life" for those who want to be his followers. The Gospels seem to indicate that Jesus thought that the kingdom was both immediate—"the kingdom of Heaven is at hand" (Matt. 10:7 KJV) and future—"when they shall see the Son of man coming in the clouds of heaven with power and great glory" (Matt. 24:30 KJV).

The First London Confession of 1644 says that the kingdom "shall be then fully perfected when he shall the second time come in glory to reign amongst his Saints, and to be admired of all them which do believe, when he shall put down all rule and authority under his feet, that the glory of the Father may be full" (Lumpkin, 162).

Many Baptists believe that it is one of the duties of baptized believers to bring persons to salvation as the first stage of their entry into the kingdom of God in this world, in preparation for the world to come. Some social gospel leaders like Baptist Walter Rauschenbusch believed that Christian action in behalf of the poor and exploited would hasten the kingdom on earth. Some Landmark Baptists believe that the local church is synonymous with the kingdom of God and bears all the necessary marks of Christ's rule and reign. For Landmarkists the local church both is the kingdom of God on earth and anticipates the kingdom that is to come. Others believe that the kingdom will come in fullness after the millennial reign of Christ and the final judgment. For all Christians, the rule and reign of God is an idea to be anticipated and proclaimed.

74. What is the nature of the final judgment?

Few, if any, of the Baptist confessions of faith neglect to address the final judgment as illustrated in the English Declaration at Amsterdam in 1611. It asserts that

> the dead shall rise again, and the living being changed in a moment, having the same bodies in substance though divers (different) in qualities, I Cor. 15:52, 38. Job 19:15–28, Luke 25: 30. That after the resurrection all men shall appear before the judgment seat of CHRIST to be judged according to their works, that the godly shall enjoy life Eternal, the wicked being condemned shall be tormented everlastingly in Hell, Matt. 25:46. (Lumpkin, 123)

Overall, contemporary Baptists would agree with that four-hundred-year-old statement. Most Baptists believe that in the end, all persons who have ever lived will stand before the "judgment seat of Christ" to be judged as to their relationship with God through Jesus Christ. Those who have not chosen or been chosen by Christ will receive condemnation as a result of their own sinful nature. Again, most Baptists would insist that the unredeemed will spend eternity in Hell, a place of torment. The redeemed, counting not on their own righteousness but on the righteousness of Christ, will spend eternity with God.

Many Baptists, especially African Americans whose heritage is that of the slave tradition, believe that the judgment seat of Christ is one where justice is set forth once and for all. That promise of justice is a powerful image in many of the black spirituals. In this view claims to Christian discipleship must be "professed" in one's treatment of other human beings. Those who claim to be followers of Christ but deny Christ's teaching to "love your neighbor as yourself" may face a different judgment than they once imagined.

75. What about death and eternity?

We all die. Confronting the reality of death is inevitable but difficult. At the foundation of Christian faith is the assertion that Christ has overcome death, not only in himself but for us. The affirmation that Christ is risen prompts St. Paul to ask, "O death where is thy sting?" (1 Cor. 15:55 KJV) The Short Confession of 1610 declares,

> We believe and teach the resurrection of the dead, both of the just and the unjust, as Paul (I Cor. 15) soundly teacheth and witnesseth: The soul shall be united to the body, every one shall be presented before the judgment seat of Christ Jesus, to receive in his own body wages according to his works. . . . The Almighty, gracious, merciful God, preserve us from the punishment of the ungodly, and grant us grace and gifts helpful to a holy life, saving death, and joyful resurrection with all the righteous. (Lumpkin, 112–13)

Baptists insist that a "personal experience with Jesus Christ" offers the gift of God that is eternal life. The Second London Confession notes that

> the Bodies of Men after Death return to dust, and see corruption; but their Souls (which neither die nor sleep) having an immortal subsistence, immediately return to God who gave them; the Souls of the Righteous being then made perfect in holiness, are received into paradise where they are with Christ, and behold the fact of God in light and glory; waiting for the full Redemption of their Bodies." (Lumpkin, 293)

This statement offers a basic summary of what would reflect the overall position of Baptists regarding death and eternity.

14

Polity

 ## 76. What is the basic form of Baptist church government?

Baptists are congregationalists in their form of church government. They believe that the authority of Jesus Christ is mediated to and through the local congregation of professed believers. The congregation, not the bishop, presbytery, or conference, speaks for Christ. That is one of Baptists' earliest and most distinctive characteristics. The English Declaration from Amsterdam in 1611 sets forth that idea as clearly as any Baptist document. It states,

> That though in respect of CHRIST, the Church be one, Ephes. 4:4, yet it consisteth of divers [many] particular congregations, even so many as there shall be in the World, every of which congregation, though they be but two or three, have CHRIST given to them, with all the means of their salvation . . . are the Body of CHRIST and a whole Church. (Lumpkin, 120)

This is another reason that the concept of a believers' church is so important to Baptists—Christ's authority is mediated through the individuals who, bound together by faith, make up Christ's body, the church. This is also the beginnings of covenant between God, the individual, and the community of faith.

In one of the most descriptive summaries of Baptist polity, the English Declaration makes the autonomy of the congregation the centerpiece of Baptist understanding of the church. It declares

> That as one congregation hath CHRIST, so hath all, 2 Cor. 10:7. And that the Word of GOD cometh not out from any one, neither to any one congregation in particular, I Cor. 14:36. But unto

every particular Church, as it doth unto all the world, Col. 1:5–6. And therefore no church ought to challenge any prerogative over any other. (Lumpkin, 120)

This is a clear statement of the autonomy of each local congregation, able to receive its own revelations directly from God and to set its own directions of ministry without any interference from other invasive congregations. While Baptists soon developed "associational" relationships between congregations, the autonomy of the congregation generally remained sacrosanct.

Baptists thus develop their church government around laity-led committees and programs. They generally organize the church according to constitutions and bylaws worked out by the congregation itself. Congregational officers—clergy and deacons—represent the two-fold ministry of the church.

 ## 77. How does Baptist congregationalism work?

Congregationalism in Baptist churches generally follows the pattern of a constitution/bylaw-based democracy. Churches develop a constitution that says how the church will be governed, establishes a committee structure for the administrative and programmatic organizations, and writes bylaws for the conduct of business. These include guidelines for the election of pastor, deacons, and other governing officers, as well as the necessary votes (majority or percentages) for selecting these officers. Most churches elect a "moderator" (sometimes the pastor, sometimes a layperson) who presides at meetings and may call special gatherings if necessary. Most Baptist churches hold periodic congregational meetings to conduct business and bring recommendations that require church votes. These meetings may be held monthly, quarterly, or annually, depending on the preference of the congregation and the rules established in the bylaws.

As noted earlier, the pastor and staff (associate pastors, if any) represent the salaried, full-time ministry base of the church. They plan and lead worship, develop and implement weekly ministries, and chart the mission of the church as acknowledged and approved by the congregation. The pastor is responsible for all aspects of the church's ministry, particularly worship leadership, preaching, and the overall "care of souls." In many larger Baptist congregations, however, associate pastors take responsibility for specific ministries, such as youth, senior adults, education, and music/worship. All may share in various aspects of pastoral care, such as hospital and home visitations, Bible teaching, and participation in worship.

Deacons, a lay office of varying number in each church, assist both pastoral staff and the church in a variety of ministries. In some congregations deacons have both administrative and spiritual duties, overseeing the work of the staff and the implementation of programs but also offering direct care to members' personal, familial, and financial needs. In other churches, the primary work of the deacons is to see to the immediate needs of members, visiting the sick and homebound, administering benevolence programs, and taking communion to those who are unable to attend church. A growing number of Baptist congregations have developed "deacon family ministries," dividing the membership among the deacons, who are then responsible for staying in touch with those families over a given period of time. Some also name "Deacons of the Week" or "Deacons on Call," who are to be contacted in case of emergencies or special familial or personal concerns. In some Baptist churches a board of trustees may oversee significant aspects of the fiscal and operational work of the church and be responsible for personnel matters, finances, audits, and upkeep on the physical plant.

78. How are pastors selected in Baptist churches?

Baptist pastors have a great deal of freedom but not a lot of job security. In a sense, Baptist ministers are "free agents," ordained by and responsible to local congregations without any churchly oversight from synods, conferences, or other ecclesiastical judicatories. Although some denominations provide official and unofficial networks that help with placement, most Baptist preachers are on their own when it comes to seeking pastoral positions, negotiating job descriptions, and connecting with the pastoral "job market." They also serve at the behest of the congregation, which means they are often only one vote away from dismissal at any given time in their ministry. In earlier eras, many Baptist ministers lived with the "annual call," a yearly vote taken by the congregation as to whether they should stay another year or be dismissed. Disputes between pastor and congregation are not uncommon in Baptist life, often resulting in dismissal of the pastor or schism in the church.

Most Baptist churches follow a congregation-based process in selecting a pastor that follows this general pattern:

1. The congregation selects a "pastor search committee" (an older term was "pulpit committee") representative of various segments of the church.
2. The committee advertises the vacancy and solicits recommendations from church leaders.
3. The committee receives and evaluates resumes from candidates and narrows the field to a list of outstanding candidates.
4. Members request audiovisual recordings of a candidate's preaching and worship leadership and/or visit the candidate's church to observe services.
5. Finalists meet with the committee and may be asked to preach "in view of a call" for the entire congregation. This step in the process varies among churches. Some bring several candidates to the congregation before the final vote (euphemistically known as a "preach-off" in some ministerial circles). Other congregations narrow the field to one candidate who is presented to the congregation. If that person fails, the committee moves to another candidate until a selection is made. Still other committees present the candidate with their recommendation but without the requisite preaching requirement before the vote.
6. The congregation votes on the candidate. Some churches require a certain percentage of the vote—simple majority, two-thirds majority, or other formulas.

Removal of a pastor often follows particular procedures set forth in the bylaws, such as review of concerns, efforts at reconciliation, and a percentage vote for removal.

79. How does one join a Baptist church?

Membership in Baptist churches revolves around several possibilities. The most basic form of membership is on the basis of "profession of faith." In this way persons acknowledge their personal experience of God's grace through Christ and request baptism into the church. In this way, profession of faith is linked with direct membership into a local Baptist congregation. Persons already baptized and holding membership in another Baptist congregation may "move their membership" to another church by attesting to earlier membership elsewhere or by requesting a formal letter of transfer from another church.

As noted earlier, nonimmersed persons who come from other Christian traditions are required by some churches to receive immersion as a prerequisite to membership. Other churches may choose to waive the baptismal requirement in favor of a simple affirmation of faith and statement of previous baptism, whatever the mode.

In some Baptist churches the membership continues a traditional practice of voting or expressing approval of the candidates for membership. Some very traditional churches ask the congregation to vote yes or no on each would-be member. In others, the vote is simply a sign of welcome for new members, given only in the affirmative. Earlier Baptists saw this congregational vote as part of the church's covenant relationship with all members and the occasion for dismissal (voting people out) if the covenant was broken.

80. What is a Baptist "association"?

Associations of Baptist churches appear early in Baptist history. These were intentional gatherings of pastors and laity from individual congregations in a given region for special services and collective ministries. Associations illustrate the fact that while Baptists have long emphasized the autonomy of the local congregation, they quickly found a mechanism for bringing churches together in cooperative, supportive endeavors. Thus they sought to strike a balance between the congregation and extended church connections. Associations began, and in many ways continue, around four basic purposes: (1) a source of fellowship and encouragement among a group of free-standing congregations; (2) a community of churches gathered around common doctrinal beliefs, affirming (and in many cases monitoring) Baptist identity together; (3) a resource for inquiries and counsel that could provide collective advice for individual churches; and (4) an opportunity to pool resources to accomplish various missions and ministries that a single congregation was not able to facilitate. In most cases associations are regional in nature, linking churches in a given geographic locale in direct ministries to grass roots clientele.

Associations are generally thought to be advisory to congregations, which in earlier times might request specific counsel regarding controversial theological or practical issues that arose in one church. Associations may also choose to dismiss congregations that step outside the majority's interpretation of Baptist doctrine. Thus some churches have been put out of their respective associational organizations for such things as ordaining women or gays, extending membership to nonimmersed Christians, certain kinds of ecumenical engagement, or other controversial stands. Nineteenth- and early twentieth-century Baptist associations often issued "circular letters" sent to member congregations and eliciting opinions from clergy and laity on specific theological topics. Today that is called blogging!

81. What is the nature of Baptist denominational structures?

From a historical perspective, Baptists have tended to mistrust "denominational alignments," fearing those "hierarchies" that might threaten or usurp power over local congregations. Yet the need for accomplishing larger ministries in response to evangelical or social imperatives threw Baptists together in organizations that became or took on varying degrees of organizational cooperation. Yet they have often remained suspicious of these overarching systems. The earliest denominational engagement came in the form of "societies" organized to address specific ministry projects and needs. In Britain and the United States Baptists formed missionary societies to fund evangelical and benevolent activities at home and abroad. The Baptist Missionary Society was founded in England in the 1790s to send William Carey and others as missionaries to India. The General Missionary Convention of the Baptist Denomination in the United States for Foreign Missions was established in 1814 to fund the work of Adoniram and Ann Hasseltine Judson in Burma. Additional societies for home missions, publication, education, and evangelism (among others) were also founded for accomplishing targeted ministries. Individuals, local churches, and associations could claim membership in those societies. Thus autonomous churches formed autonomous societies.

With the founding of the Southern Baptist Convention in 1845, the convention system became a more elaborate model for denominational cooperation. In this system, denominational agencies (societies) were closely linked through the overarching convention, with trustees of boards appointed by the convention, not by the individual society. Ultimately, a collective funding mechanism was developed that divided total funds given through the denomination between the diverse boards and agencies. The convention system linked autonomous churches, associations, and state Baptist conventions in an overall denominational program and identity. From the late nineteenth through the twentieth century, Baptists have formed a variety of conventions, with varying degrees of organizational structure. These include various African American–based "National Baptist" groups and the American Baptist Churches in the U.S.A., among others.

Other Baptist groups reacted vehemently against these connectional systems, retaining primary alliance to and connection with local churches. Mission and evangelistic work is accomplished through direct funding from local congregations rather than from what seemed to many to be "unscriptural" boards. These churches have sometimes founded "fellowships" of pastors for mutual encouragement, placement, and evangelism. These include more fundamentalist-based groups such as the Southwide Baptist Fellowship and the Baptist Bible Fellowship, as well as Landmark groups such as the American Baptist Association and the Baptist Missionary Association.

82. Might Baptists ever have bishops?

Early Baptists may have used the title "bishop" as a term for those who occupied the pastoral office, using it interchangeably with the term elder or pastor. More recently, however, especially among some African American Baptists, "bishop" is being used to designate "prelates" who have extraordinary leadership roles over one or more Baptist congregations. Some pastors of megachurches have also begun to use the title.

Other Baptists would soundly reject this approach to Baptist leadership as a return to a form of ecclesiastical hierarchy against which the earliest Baptists strongly reacted. It promises to raise serious questions about Baptist identity, history, and future, especially if the consecration of bishops becomes anything like normative in Baptist life.

83. May women serve as pastors of Baptist churches?

The answer to that question depends on the specific Baptist church. In some Baptist churches women serve as pastors and other staff members. They are ordained to the "gospel ministry" and fulfill all the pastoral and spiritual functions of any pastor, male or female. While this development did not occur in any significant numbers in Baptist churches until the later twentieth century, it is now increasingly normative in certain segments of Baptist church life. These churches believe that the freedom of the gospel opens the door to the calling of women and men to all facets of church life, that the Spirit was poured out on "all flesh" at Pentecost, enabling "your sons and your daughters" to "prophesy" (Acts 2:17). Yes, Baptist polity and theology in *some* Baptist congregations permits and extends the pastoral call to female ministers.

In other Baptist congregations and denominational groups (a majority, no doubt) the ordination of women to the ministry and the calling of women as pastors is strictly forbidden on the basis of a variety of texts, including several in 1 Timothy, such as the admonition that the "bishop" (pastor) is to be the "husband of one wife," (1 Tim. 3:2 KJV) and the passage "But I suffer not a woman to teach, nor to usurp authority over the man, but to be in silence" (1 Tim. 2:12 KJV). No, Baptist polity and theology in *some* Baptist churches excludes women from ordination or calling to the pastoral office.

Baptist polity, however, means that a local church has the freedom to ordain or not to ordain women to ministry according to the members' own understanding of Scripture, history, and conscience, actions that may break fellowship with other Baptist individuals and groups. This issue no doubt will continue to divide Baptist churches and Baptist men and women for years to come.

84. What is the future of Baptist polity and identity?

𝒜s the twenty-first century moves forward, Baptists find themselves confronting a variety of issues regarding Baptist identity in general and polity in particular. Some Baptist congregations are minimizing the name Baptist in their own self-identification; others are moving toward a more Presbyterian system of polity that minimizes congregation church government and gives more authority to presbytery-like, representative governance. We have already noted that a small but significant group of churches have begun to consecrate and unite around bishops, a major departure from historical Baptist practices. Many clergy and laity alike express their own fatigue at the cumbersome, often troublesome and confrontational nature of congregational polity and its tendency to divide and split communities of faith as easily as it can bind them together.

At the same time, contemporary society needs faith communities that continue to reflect the church of Jesus Christ as a peoples' movement, giving voice to multiple views and opening the door to diversity and openness in the new community of the church. The genius and hope of the Baptists remains much as it was with the little group in Amsterdam four hundred years ago, with their audacious idea that the people can be trusted to interpret Scripture aright, in the context of a believing community and under the guidance of the Holy Spirit.

For Further Reading

Bettenson, Henry, ed. *Documents of the Christian Church.* London: Oxford University Press, 1963.

Brackney, William H. *The Baptists.* New York: Greenwood Press, 1988.

———, ed. *Baptist Life and Thought, 1600–1980.* Valley Forge, PA: Judson Press, 1983.

———. *A Genetic History of Baptist Thought.* Macon, GA: Mercer University Press, 2004.

Dorgan, Howard. *Giving Glory to God in Appalachia: Worship Practices of Six Baptist Subdenominations.* Knoxville: University of Tennessee Press, 1987.

Durso, Keith. *No Armor for the Back: Baptist Prison Writings, 1600s–1700s.* Macon, GA: Mercer University Press, 2007.

Fiddes, Paul S. *Tracks and Traces: Baptist Identity in Church and Theology.* Waynesboro, GA: Paternoster Press, 2004.

Fitts, Leroy. *A History of Black Baptists.* Nashville: Broadman Press: 1985.

Freeman, Curtis, James William McLendon Jr., and C. Rosalee Velloso da Silva. *Baptist Roots: A Reader in the Theology of a Christian People.* Valley Forge, PA: Judson Press, 1999.

Gardner, Robert. *Baptists in Early America: A Statistical History, 1639–1790.* Atlanta: Georgia Baptist Historical Society, 1983.

Goodwin, Everett C., ed. *Baptists in the Balance.* Valley Forge, PA: Judson Press, 1997.

Helwys, Thomas. *A Short Declaration of the Mystery of Iniquity.* Ed. Richard Groves. Macon, GA: Mercer University Press, 1993.

Higginbotham, Evelyn Brooks. *Righteous Discontent: The Women's Movement in the Black Baptist Church, 1880–1920.* Cambridge, MA: Harvard University Press, 1993.

Jonas, Glenn. *The Baptist River.* Macon, GA: Mercer University Press, 2006.

Leonard, Bill J. *Baptists in America.* New York: Columbia University Press, 2005.

———. *Baptist Ways: A History.* Valley Forge, PA: Judson Press, 2003.

———. *A Dictionary of Baptists in America.* Downers Grove, IL: InterVarsity Press, 1994.

Lumpkin, William L. *Baptist Confessions of Faith.* Valley Forge, PA: Judson Press, 1974.

Maring, Norman, and Winthrop Hudson. *A Baptist Manual of Polity and Practice*. Rev. ed. Valley Forge, PA: Judson Press, 1991.

Martin, Sandy D. *Black Baptists and African Missions*. Macon, GA: Mercer University Press, 1989.

McBeth, H. Leon. *The Baptist Heritage*. Nashville: Broadman Press, 1987.

———. *A Sourcebook for Baptist Heritage*. Nashville: Broadman Press, 1990.

Smith, H. Shelton, Robert T. Handy, and Lefferts A. Loetscher, eds. *American Christianity: An Historical Interpretation with Representative Documents*. 2 vols. New York: Charles Scribner's Sons, 1963.

Stanley, Bryan. *The History of the Baptist Missionary Society, 1792–1992*. Edinburgh: T. & T. Clark, 1992.

Wardin, Albert W., ed. *Baptists around the World: A Comprehensive Handbook*. Nashville: Broadman & Holman, 1995.

Printed in the USA
CPSIA information can be obtained
at www.ICGtesting.com
BVHW031315250823
668881BV00003B/63

9 780664 232894